The Wisdom of the
SAINTS

The Wisdom of the SAINTS

EDITED BY SUZANNE CLORES

PHILOSOPHICAL LIBRARY

CITADEL PRESS
Kensington Publishing Corp.
www.kensingtonbooks.com

CITADEL PRESS BOOKS are published by

Kensington Publishing Corp.
850 Third Avenue
New York, NY 10022

Copyright © 2002 Suzanne Clores

All rights reserved. No part of this book may be reproduced in any form or by any means without the prior written consent of the publisher, excepting brief quotes used in reviews.

Titles included in the Wisdom Library are published by arrangement with Philosophical Library.

All Kensington titles, imprints, and distributed lines are available at special quantity discounts for bulk purchases for sales promotions, premiums, fund-raising, educational, or institutional use. Special book excerpts or customized printings can also be created to fit specific needs. For details, write or phone the office of the Kensington special sales manager: Kensington Publishing Corp., 850 Third Avenue, New York, NY 10022, attn: Special Sales Department, phone 1-800-221-2647.

CITADEL PRESS is Reg. U.S. Pat. & TM Off.
The Citadel Logo is a trademark of Kensington Publishing Corp.

First Wisdom Library printing: August 2002

10 9 8 7 6 5 4 3 2 1

Printed in the United States of America

Library of Congress Control Number: 2002105468

ISBN 0-8065-2391-3

I dedicate this book to the Saints themselves and to all who have benefited from their guidance.

The influence of genuine saints is not limited to their own time and place but seems to go out in waves, not only to different places but different times.
—Dan Wakefield

CONTENTS

Introduction	xi
Section One—Freedom	3
Section Two—Peace	13
Section Three—Fear and Protection	21
Section Four—Compassion (Forgiveness of Sins)	35
Section Five—Politics	45
Section Six—Love	55
Section Seven—The Physical Body	63
Section Eight—Service	75
Section Nine—Indecision	85
Section Ten—Disease/Healing	93
Section Eleven—Education	103
Section Twelve—Money	113
Section Thirteen—Hope	121
Biographical Notes on the Sources	131
Bibliography	155

INTRODUCTION

We have always looked to the saints for advice. These blessed men and women offer us the peace of mind that comes from divine knowledge, answers when we are uncertain, and security when we feel unsafe. The saints use words to teach us how to face the fearful challenges we face daily. Who are these wise people and how do they help us to lead better lives? One conventional definition of sainthood requires proof that an individual has performed a miracle. But the definition used in this book is broader, more ecumenical. The saints we hear from in these pages speak out of many religious traditions, though mainly from the Western Christian church. Also quoted are sages of the East, surely no less loving and wise, and similarly deserving of the honor of sainthood, albeit less "official" than that bestowed by the Church. Whether sages from the streets of India or intellectual friends of the Pope, saints' messages are the same: Love each other, love God.

Religions around the world have their own processes of recognizing and naming a saint. Catholicism recognizes saints by exaltation processes like canonization and beatification. Ancient Jewish sages are members of a tradition that values the wisdom of righteousness, and men such as Maimonides can surely be called saintly. The Eastern religions permit a still more flexible definition of sainthood. Poets, teachers, sages, monks, and sometimes even "madmen" contributed some of the holiest words and passages of wisdom to the Eastern canon. The bodhisattva in Buddhist tradition is one who reaches enlightenment, but who remains on the wheel of samsara (rebirth and death, again and again) in order to serve humanity; a saintly act indeed, and so the words of Buddhist teachers such as Tilopa, Naropa, and Milarepa can be found in the following pages. Hinduism calls for no formal process beyond an individual's saintly works and the acknowledgment of them by devotees; among the saints included here are beloved Hindus such as Swami Vivekananda, poet Mira Bai, and holy man Rama Krishna.

For our purposes, then, saints are people beyond the institution of religion. We may even think of them as otherworldly, but in fact, many were well grounded in their humanity. Many, also, were angry about the state of affairs of their day, and some were sufficiently outraged to turn away from God. Dorothy Day, founder of the *Catholic Worker* and well on her way to becoming canonized, asked early on in her career, "Where were the saints to try to change the social order, not just to minister to the slaves, but to do away with slavery?" Words like these are stirring and can inspire us to act to better our lives and the lives of others.

No matter what their individual religion may be, all the saints quoted here have devoted their lives to the spiritual and to transmitting their knowledge of it to the rest of us. People have always craved the spiritual and spiritual guidance. We need to know how to cope with the corruption in business and government that causes so much suffering. We need consolation in times of chaos, war, and violence. And we are fortunate to find saints in the midst of it all, individuals to whom we can look for inspiration, verification that we are spiritual beings too, who can learn perfect love in this lifetime. Whatever their faith, saints have listened closely to God and can bring us holy messages of comfort and inspiration.

The following thirteen sections, divided by subject, provide saintly commentary on elements of human life to challenge and inspire us.

As Saint Teresa of Avila said, "The important thing is not to think much, but to love much and so do that which best stirs you to love." Her primary message, and that of all the saints quoted here, is that we must awaken to love. We need their words to help us to do it.

The Wisdom of the
SAINTS

Section One

FREEDOM

The word freedom has powerful connotations. We see freedom as our birthright, a way to behave without inhibition. To the spiritually minded in almost every discipline, freedom is also our inherent nature, but because we are mortal, we are separate from the true experience of being free. To regain freedom, we must spend time with God.

Concerning jealous folk, however, whom you have endured till now as accusers and plotters, I tell you what you already know: that vice always envies virtue. If you want to be free of the persecution of jealousy, therefore, either find a place where you can hide concealed from wicked people, or renounce virtues. But you will do neither of these, because one is impossible and the other detestable. All that remains for you is, armed with the arms of justice at the right and at the left, to pass over with the Apostle through glory and dishonor, through disgrace and good reputation; and whatever these folk plot, direct your thoughts never to them but with a strong calm mind to your own steps.
—Saint Anselm of Canterbury

When I hear your words, I am both full and hungry; full, because nothing delights me except your words; hungry, because the more I hear them the more fervently I want them. Therefore, blissful God, give me help always to do your will.
—Saint Birgitta

On the 4th of July

> Behold, the dark clouds melt away,
> That gathered thick at night, and hung
> So like a gloomy pall above the earth!
>
> Before thy magic touch, the world
> Awakes. The birds in chorus sing.
> The flowers raise their star-like crowns
> Dew-set, and wave thee welcome fair.

The lakes are opening wide in love
Their hundred thousand lotus-eyes
To welcome thee, with all their depth.

All hail to thee, thou Lord of Light!
A welcome new to thee, today,
O sun! today thou sheddest LIBERTY!
Bethink thee how the world did wait,
And search for thee, through time and clime.

Some gave up home and love of friends,
And went in quest of thee, self banished,
Through dreary oceans, through primeval forests,
Each step a struggle for their life or death;

Then came the day when work bore fruit,
And worship, love, and sacrifice,
Fulfilled, accepted, and complete.
Then thou, propitious, rose to shed
The light of FREEDOM on mankind.

Move on, O Lord, on thy resistless path!
Till thy high noon o'erspreads the world.
Till every land reflects thy light,
Till men and women, with uplifted head,
Behold their shackles broken, and
Know, in springing joy, their life renewed!
—Swami Vivekananda

On the 4th of July 1898, Swami Vivekananda was traveling with some American disciples in Kashmir, and as part of a celebration of the anniversary of their Declaration of Independence, he prepared the preceding poem to be read aloud at the day's early breakfast.

Free your mind from all that troubles you; God will take care of things. You will be unable to make haste in this (choice) without, so to speak, grieving the heart of God, be-

cause he sees that you do not honor him sufficiently with holy trust. Trust in him, I beg you, and you will have the fulfillment of what your heart desires.
—Saint Vincent de Paul

No chains of slavery are stronger than those of passion.
—Edith Stein

It is really a perfect misery to be alive when we have always to be going about like men with enemies at their gates, who cannot lay aside their arms even when sleeping or eating, and are always afraid of being surprised by a breaching of their fortress in some weak spot.
—Saint Teresa of Avila

If a light does not differ from another light, is not more or less intense than the other, we do not say that it is the same light; each one has its own precise Being; but we do say that it is exactly and invariably similar in Being.
—Saint Basil the Great

I want to console You for the ingratitude of the wicked, and I beg of You to take away my freedom to displease You. If through weakness I sometimes fall, may Your Divine Glance cleanse my soul immediately, consuming all my imperfections like the fire that transforms everything into itself.
—Saint Thérèse of Lisieux

Peter said of the slaves: "We must speak to them with our hands by giving, before we try to speak to them with our lips."
—Saint Peter Claver

Saint Catherine has told me that I shall have help; I do not know if this will be delivery from prison, or if, whilst I am being tried, some disturbance may happen, by which I shall be delivered. The help will come to me, I think, in one way or the other. Besides this, my Voices have told me that I shall be delivered by a great victory; and they add: "Be resigned; have no care for thy martyrdom; you will come in the end to the Kingdom of Paradise." They have told me this simply, absolutely, and without fail. What is meant by my martyrdom is the pain and adversity that I suffer in prison; I do not know if I shall have still greater suffering to bear; for that I refer me to God.

—Saint Joan of Arc

In the future, be made powerful in the Lord, and in the might of his strength. Put on the whole armour of God, that ye may be able to stand against the wiles of the devil. Because our wrestling is not against blood and flesh, but against the principalities, against the powers, against the world rulers of this darkness, against the spiritual forces of wickedness in the heavenly order.

—Saint Luke
Epistle to the Ephesians

The following quote comes from correspondence between Naropa, a Tibetan student, and Tilopa, a Tibetan teacher, who both lived during the tenth century. In the Buddhist tradition, freedom comes with exiting the ocean of samsara, the word for the cycle of birth and death in which all humans are caught.

When I depend on the ship, the Guru, the precious
Jewel of the Mind, I am sure of freedom
From Samsara's ocean. This practice teaches that the path towards maturity is bliss.

Tilopa said:
You seem still to be attracted by the teaching
Of the Guru who understands reality as bliss.
Your emotions still seem to be unstable since you hanker
After the instruction on the profound meaning of reality
By the Guru who understands it as bliss in blissfulness.
Hanker not for this nor for its opposite.
—Naropa and Tilopa
from letters

Be not fearful of the flesh, nor love it.
If thou fear before it, it will become
master over thee. If thou love it, it will swallow and
paralyse thee.
—Philip the Gnostic
The Gospel of Philip

If a man wishes to take your coat, give him also whatever other article of clothes you have.
—Augustine of Hippo

Every Holy Mass, heard with devotion, produces in our souls marvelous effects, abundant spiritual and material graces which we, ourselves, do not know. . . . It is easier for the earth to exist without the sun than without the Holy Sacrifice of the Mass!
—Padre Pio

Christ is both the way and the door. Christ is the staircase and the vehicle, like the "throne of mercy over the Ark of the Covenant," and "the mystery hidden from the ages." A man should turn his full attention to this throne of mercy, and should gaze at him hanging on the cross, full of faith, hope, and charity, devoted, full of wonder and joy, marked

by gratitude, and open to praise and jubilation. Then such a man will make with Christ a "pasch," that is, a passing-over. Through the branches of the cross he will pass over the Red Sea, leaving Egypt and entering the desert. There he will taste the hidden manna, and rest with Christ in the sepulcher, as if he were dead to things outside. He will experience, as much as is possible for one who is still living, what was promised to the thief who hung beside Christ: "Today you will be with me in paradise."
—Saint Bonaventure
from *Journey of the Mind to God*

He who has yet to master Self-Awareness
Should not expect freedom from ghosts and Devas.
—Milarepa

It must not be supposed that the heavens or the luminaries are endowed with life. For they are inanimate and insensible. So that when the divine Scripture saith, Let the heavens rejoice and the earth be glad, it is the angels in heaven and the men on earth that are invited to rejoice. For the Scripture is familiar with the figure of personification, and is wont to speak of inanimate things as though they were animate: for example, The sea saw it and fled: Jordan was driven back. And again, What ailed thee, O thou sea, that thou fleddest? Thou, O Jordan, that thou was driven back? Mountains, too, and hills are asked the reason of their leaping in the same way as we are wont to say, the city was gathered together, when we do not mean the buildings, but the inhabitants of the city: again, the heavens declare the glory of God, does not mean that they send forth a voice that can be heard by bodily ears, but that from their own greatness they bring before our minds the power of the Creator: and when we contemplate their beauty we praise the Maker as the Master-Craftsman.
—Saint John of Damascus

The soul, who is lifted by a very great and yearning desire for the honor of God and the salvation of souls, begins by exercising herself, for a certain space of time, in the ordinary virtues, remaining in the cell of self-knowledge, in order to know better the goodness of God towards her. This she does because knowledge must precede love, and only when she has attained love, can she strive to follow and to clothe herself with the truth. But, in no way, does the creature receive such a taste of the truth, or so brilliant a light therefrom, as by means of humble and continuous prayer, founded on knowledge of herself and of God; because prayer, exercising her in the above way, unites with God the soul that follows the footprints of Christ Crucified, and thus, by desire and affection, and union of love, makes her another Himself.

—Saint Catherine of Siena
from *On Divine Providence*

When a man gives up all desires
that emerge from the mind, and rests
contented in the Self by the Self,
he is called a man of firm wisdom.

He whose mind is untroubled
by any misfortune, whose craving
for pleasures has disappeared,
who is free from greed, fear, anger,

who is unattached to all things,
who neither grieves nor rejoices
if good or if bad things happen—
that man is a man of firm wisdom.

—Bhagavad Gita

Theologians debate situation ethics and the new morality (leaving out of account the problem of means and ends) while the screams of the flaming human torches, civilian and soldiers, rise high to heaven. The only conclusion I have ever been able to reach is that we must pray God to increase our faith, a faith without which one cannot love or hope. "Lord, I believe, help thou my unbelief."

—Dorothy Day

The only true sacrifice to offer God, O lovers of God, the only authentic renunciation that can clear away obstacles to spiritual porgies, is to abandon once and for all this constant drive for self-perpetuation, this instinctive urge to survive and dominate which manifests in so many subtle and obvious forms—including the obsession with becoming holy or elevated.

—Sri Ramakrishna

Children of the world say they are free when they are not subject to another's will, when no one stops them from satisfying their wishes and inclinations. For this dream of freedom, they engage in bloody battles and sacrifice life and limb. The children of God see freedom as something else. They want to be unhindered in following the Spirit of God; and they know that the greatest hindrances do not come from without, but lie within us ourselves.

—Edith Stein

Section Two

PEACE

In times of uncertainty we are drawn to think of peace as a state of behavior between nations, between people. Rarely do we think of achieving a state of peace within ourselves, the process often seems so daunting and abstract. Saints have spent their lives seeking inner peace, which they've discerned comes from spending time in conversation with God. The Eastern traditions tell us that gazing inward will show us the direction to peace. The saints of Christianity knew that true divinity dwelled within a realm known as Peace. Christ himself was known as the Prince of Peace, the savior who would deliver human kind from evil. The wisdom here reminds us that peace, whether a state of the world or a state of a human being, is also a state of mind.

That where there should be the lovely feet of those who bear the torch of the Gospel peace, there may not be the dark and wandering footsteps of apostates, but that when our loins are girded the Father all-merciful may put blazing torches in our hands to enlighten the hearts of the Gentiles to the vision of the Gospel of the Glory of Christ.
—Saint Boniface

Have patience in persevering in the holy exercise of meditation, and be content to progress in slow steps until you have legs to run and wings with which to fly.
—Padre Pio

My life is of no value . . . I can offer it in peace.
—Blessed Maria Gabriella

For peace and freedom are not otherwise won, than by ceaseless and unyielding struggles with our lusts.
—Saint Clement of Alexandria

In that (divine) state I see myself as alone with God, totally cleansed, totally sanctified, totally true, totally upright, totally certain, totally celestial in him. And when I am in that state, I do not remember anything else . . . When I leave that supreme state in which I do not remember anything else, I come back and see myself in those good things I have just spoken about, but at the same time I see myself completely full of sin and obedient to it, devious, impure, totally false and erroneous, and yet I am in a state of quiet. For what remains with me is a continual divine unction, the highest of

all and superior to any I have ever experienced in all my life.
—Angela of Foligno

But we are not blissfully safe, in having of our endless joy, till we be all in peace and in love: that is to say, full pleased with God and with all His works, and with all His judgments, and loving and peaceable with our self and with our even-Christians and with all that God loveth, as love beseemeth. And this doeth God's Goodness in us.
—Julian of Norwich

I would say that we are living in a hard school where from day to day there is a war going on in which we can only use the weapons of the spirit, and try to practice the non-violence we talk so much about.
—Dorothy Day

> Peace
> Behold, it comes in might,
> The power that is not power,
> The light that is in darkness,
> The shade in dazzling light.
>
> It is joy that never spoke,
> And grief unfelt, profound,
> Immortal life unlived,
> Eternal death unmourned.
>
> It is not joy nor sorrow,
> But that which is between,
> It is not night nor morrow,
> But that which joins them in.
> —Swami Vivekananda

For he is our peace, which has made of both one, and has broken down the wall that was a stop between us, and has also put away through his flesh, the cause of hatred (that is to say, the law of commandments contained in the law written) for to make of two one new man in himself, so making peace.
—Saint Luke
Epistle to the Ephesians

It follows that the perfect peacemaking is that which keeps unchanged in all circumstances what is peaceful; calls Providence holy and good; and has its being in the knowledge of divine and human affairs, by which it deems the opposites that are in the world to be the fairest harmony of creation. They also are peacemakers, who teach those who war against the stratagems of sin to have recourse to faith and peace.
—Clement of Alexandria

There must be diversity in the divine vision, in that some see the divine substance more perfectly, some less perfectly. Hence, in order to indicate this difference in happiness, our Lord says, (John 14:2): "In my father's house, there are many mansions."
—Saint Thomas Aquinas

In the last few months one has often heard the complaint that the many prayers for peace are still without effect. What right have we to be heard? Our desire for peace is undoubtedly genuine and sincere. But does it come from a completely purified heart?
—Edith Stein

Heavenly Father, you have given us a model of life in the Holy Family of Nazareth. Help us, O loving Father to make our family another Nazareth where love, peace and joy reign. May it be deeply contemplative, intensely Eucharistic and vibrant with joy.

Help us to stay together in joy and sorrow through family prayer. Teach us to see Jesus in the members of our family especially in their distressing disguise. May the Eucharistic Heart of Jesus make our hearts meek and humble like His and help us to carry out our family duties in a holy way.

May we love one another as God loves each one of us more and more each day, and forgive each other's faults as You forgive our sins.

Help us, O loving Father to take whatever You give and to give whatever You take with a big smile.

Immaculate Heart of Mary, cause of our joy, pray for us. Saint Joseph, pray for us. Holy Guardian Angels be always with us, guide and protect us. Amen.
—Prayer by Mother Teresa of Calcutta

Sanctify yourself and you will sanctify society.
—Saint Francis of Assisi

I would like the angels of Heaven to be among us. I would like an abundance of peace. I would like full vessels of charity. I would like rich treasures of mercy. I would like cheerfulness to preside over all. I would like Jesus to be present. I would like the three Marys of illustrious renown to be with us. I would like the friends of Heaven to be gathered around us from all parts. I would like myself to be a rent payer to the Lord; that I should suffer distress, that he would bestow a good blessing upon me. I would like a great lake of beer for the King of Kings. I would like to be watching Heaven's family drinking it through all eternity.
—Saint Brigid

Prayer to Immaculate Mary

Give me the grace to annihilate my will before the Will of Your Divine Son so that the Will of Your Divine Son be mine. Kindle my heart with Divine Love! See to it that the purest flame of God's Love penetrate deeply in my spirit and rout out my selfishness. Give me a tender devotion to the Blessed Sacrament and Your holy Love in order that I love You as You deserve. Help me detach perfectly from everything, creatures, and myself, renouncing myself and everything to live only in God. My tender Mother, obtain for me a deep humility from God, internal and external humility, a deep knowledge of myself, and a spirit of mortification so that I humble myself before God and creatures. Help me to have contempt and humiliations loved, but myself despised. Mirror of humility grant me the virtue of humility and obedience. Grant me the virtue of meekness and sweetness so that I treat people with kindness, especially when I meet the ones against whom I feel repugnance. Give me a simple, merry, sweet, gentle, kind, benign, compassionate, humble and meek heart. Impetrate for me a profound contrition and intimate sorrow to make my heart bleed for my offenses against Your Divine Son. Grant me a spirit of holy prayer, the grace of meditating upon the sublime truths of faith, especially the Passion of Jesus and Your sorrows. Give me the grace of praying in the occasions of sin. Grant me a holy recollection, the grace of being aware of Your holy presence, and the virtue of silence. Grant me from God the holy virtue of spiritual and bodily purity; as well as purity of conscience through humble, frequent, and sincere confession, for the greater glory of God. Obtain for me a heroic faith along with a loving, filial confidence in the Most Sacred Heart of Jesus and in Your Motherly affection. Grant me fervent zeal for the glory of God and the salvation of souls, letting me perform the duties of my priestly min-

istry perfectly. See to it that I celebrate the Holy Sacrifice of the Mass and recite the Holy Canonical Hours with deep recollection and intimate devotion. My tender Mother, give me the virtue of fortitude to prevail over myself through internal and external mortification. O valiant Lady, you have conquered hell. Give me strength to triumph over the devil, the world, and the flesh. You are our life and hope, please grant me holy, final perseverance in the grace of Your Divine Son. See to it that I live and die saintly, and love You in Paradise forever.
—Blessed Father Annibale Di Francia

> He who clings not now to things,
> Will in his next life be joyful.
> One who has little arrogance,
> Will be loved by all
> —Milarepa

> The undisciplined have no wisdom,
> no one-pointed concentration;
> with no concentration, no peace;
> with no peace, where can joy be?
> —Bhagavad Gita

Section Three

FEAR AND PROTECTION

Psalm 23 reminds us that fear is an enemy against which we must constantly fight, and the most effective way to fight that enemy is to ask for God's protection. To remember, "the Lord is my shepherd, I shall not want" is to remember that God guides us at all times. He will provide us with the tools and the safety that we need in order to survive. Surrendering in times of fear may at first be thought of as cowardly. But from a divine point of view, surrendering in times of fear means surrender to the unknown because your trust in God will carry you. "While I walk through the valley of the shadow of death, I fear no evil. Thy rod and Thy staff, they comfort me." Plenty of saints surrendered to dismal circumstances—physical pain, poverty, psychological discomfort and emotional loneliness—because they knew that God would see them through their fear.

That where there should be the lovely feet of those who bear the torch of the Gospel peace, there may not be the dark and wandering footsteps of apostates, but that when our loins are girded the Father all-merciful may put blazing torches in our hands to enlighten the hearts of the Gentiles to the vision of the Gospel of the Glory of Christ.
—Saint Boniface

When we fly from Thee, Thou pursuest us; when we turn our backs, Thou dost present thyself before us; when we despise Thee, Thou dost entreat us; and there is neither insult nor contempt which hinders Thee from labouring unwearied to bring us to the attainment of that which eye hath not seen, nor ear heard, and which the heart of man cannot comprehend.
—Saint Bernard

We know, in fact, that it is safer for a man to flee such a burden as much as possile, fearing his weakness, than lightly to take it on his shoulders, trusting in his strength. But since it is written, "No one lives for himself, and no one dies for himself but whether we live or whether we die, we are the Lord's"; thus we ought so to walk in the path of righteousness between the fear of our own weakness and obedience to the Lord's will that we are seen to disregard neither.
—Saint Anselm of Canterbury

Through fear, some souls grow slack in their prayer—which is what the devil wants—in order to struggle against these movements, and others give it up entirely, for they think these feelings come while they are engaged in prayer rather than at other times. And this is true because the devil excites these feelings while souls are at prayer, instead of when they are engaged in other works, so that they might abandon prayer.

—Saint John of the Cross

Psalm 23

1. The Lord is my shepherd, I shall not want.
2. He makes me lie down in green pastures;
   he leads me beside still waters;
3. he restores my soul.
   He leads me in right paths for His name's sake.
4. Even though I walk through the darkest valley,
   I fear no evil;
   for you are with me; your rod and your staff—
   they comfort me.
5. You prepare a table before me
   in the presence of my enemies;
   You anoint my head with oil; my cup overflows.
6. Surely goodness and mercy shall follow me
   all the days of my life,
   and I shall dwell in the house of the Lord my whole
   life long.

—Bible

Let nothing trouble you, let nothing make you afraid. All things pass away. God never changes. Patience obtains everything. God alone is enough.

—Saint Teresa of Avila

And how are we able to react after the instinctive motions of righteous wrath are under control? Our only guide is first of all our common sense, which tells us to put a lock on our gas tank for instance, and to keep the check book locked

away safely, and not to put occasions of sin in the path of the weak. And then we are to go by the light of faith and the Old as well as the New Testament is our guide.
—Dorothy Day

As, however, fear itself is the beginning of wisdom and the source of blessedness—for they that fear the Lord are blessed—he has plainly marked himself out as the teacher for instruction in wisdom, and the guide to the attainment of blessedness.
—Saint Ambrose, Bishop of Milan
from *Three Books on the Duties of the Clergy*

To avoid dissentions we should be ever on our guard, more especially with those who drive us to argue with them, with those who vex and irritate us, and who say things likely to excite us to anger. When we find ourselves in company with quarrelsome, eccentric individuals, people who openly and unblushingly say the most shocking things, difficult to put up with, we should take refuge in silence, and the wisest plan is not to reply to people whose behavior is so preposterous.

Those who insult us and treat us contumeliously are anxious for a spiteful and sarcastic reply: the silence we then affect disheartens them, and they cannot avoid showing their vexation; they do all they can to provoke us and to elicit a reply, but the best way to baffle them is to say nothing, refuse to argue with them, and to leave them to chew the cud of their hasty anger. This method of bringing down their pride disarms them, and shows them plainly that we slight and despise them.
—Saint Ambrose, Bishop of Milan
from *Offices*

Christ shield me this day:
   Christ with me,
   Christ before me,
   Christ behind me,
   Christ in me,
   Christ beneath me,
   Christ above me,
   Christ on my right,
   Christ on my left,
   Christ when I lie down,
   Christ when I arise,
   Christ in the heart of every person who thinks of me,
   Christ in every eye that sees me,
   Christ in the ear that hears me
—Saint Patrick
from his breastplate

   That dark Dweller in Braj
   Is my only refuge.
   O my companion,
   Worldly comfort is an illusion,
   As soon you get it, it goes.
   I have chosen the Indestructible for my refuge,
   Him whom the snake of death
   Will not devour.
   My Beloved dwells in my heart,
   I have actually seen that Abode of Joy.
   Mira's Lord is Hari, the Indestructible.
   My Lord, I have taken refuge with Thee,
   Thy slave.
—Mira Bai

Jesus Christ my God, I adore you and I thank you for all the graces you have given me this day.

I offer you my sleep and all the moments of this night, and I implore you to keep me safe from sin
To this end I place myself in your sacred side and under the mantle of our Lady, my Mother. Let your holy angels surround me and keep me in peace; and let your blessing be upon me.
Amen.
—Saint Alphonsus de Liguori

I am more afraid of those who are terrified of the devil than I am of the devil himself.
—Saint Teresa of Avila

Wherefore the divine law appears to me necessarily to menace with fear, that, by caution and attention, the philosopher may acquire and retain absence of anxiety, continuing without fall and without sin in all things.
—Saint Clement of Alexandria

We must fear God out of love, not love Him out of fear.
—Saint Francis de Sales

You know to what extent the Torah lays stress upon love: with all thy heart, and with all thy soul, and with all thy might (Deuteronomy 6:5). For these two ends, namely love and fear, are achieved through two things: love through the opinions taught by the law, which include the apprehension of his being as He, may He be exalted, is in truth; while fear is achieved by means of all actions proscribed by the Law, as we have explained.
—Maimonides

I would have you draw from your monastic vow not pride but fear. You walk laden with gold; you must keep out of

the robber's way. To us men this life is a race-course we contend here, we are crowned elsewhere. No man can lay aside fear while serpents and scorpions beset his path. The Lord says: "My sword hath drunk its fill in heaven," and do you expect to find peace on the earth? No, the earth yields only thorns and thistles, and its dust is food for the serpent. "For our wrestling is not against flesh and blood, but against the principalities, against the powers, against the world-rulers of this darkness, against the spiritual hosts of wickedness in the heavenly places." We are hemmed in by hosts of foes, our enemies are upon every side. The weak flesh will soon be ashes: one against many, it fights against tremendous odds. Not till it has been dissolved, not till the Prince of this world has come and found no sin therein, not till then may you safely listen to the prophet's words: "Thou shall not be afraid for the terror by night nor for the arrow that flieth by day; nor for the trouble which haunteth thee in darkness; nor for the demon and his attacks at noonday. A thousand shall fall at thy side and ten thousand at thy right hand; but it shall not come nigh thee." When the hosts of the enemy distress you, when your frame is fevered and your passions roused, when you say in your heart, "What shall I do?" Elisha's words shall give you your answer, "Fear not, for they that be with us are more than they that be with them."
—Saint Jerome
from Letter 23 to Eustochium

My View on Reality is perfected in three aspects,
With it I overwhelm the Hinayana teaching.
To describe this with a simile,
'Tis like a fearless lion strutting in the snow—
Blessed and joyful is my mind.

My Practice of Skill and Wisdom
Is like an eagle's mighty wings

With which I soar into the firmament.
I fly through the sky without fear of falling—
Blessed and joyful is my mind.

My action is full of strength and valor,
Both distractions and drowsiness are destroyed.
To describe this with a parable,
'Tis like a tiger stalking through
The woods without fear or dread—
Blessed and joyful is my mind!
—Milarepa

For all things which are not in our hands He hath predetermined by His foreknowledge, each in its own proper and peculiar time and place.
—Saint John of Damascus

The Litany of the Fourteen Holy Helpers

LORD, have mercy on us.
Christ, have mercy on us.
Lord, have mercy on us.
Christ, hear us.
Christ, graciously hear us.
God the Father of Heaven,
Have mercy on us.
God the Son, Redeemer of the world,
Have mercy on us.
God the Holy Ghost,
Have mercy on us.
Holy Trinity, one God,
Have mercy on us.
Holy Mary, Queen of Martyrs,
pray for us.
Saint Joseph, helper in all needs, etc.
Fourteen Holy Helpers,

Saint George, valiant Martyr of Christ,
Saint Blase, zealous bishop and benefactor of the poor,
Saint Erasmus, mighty protector of the oppressed,
Saint Pantaleon, miraculous exemplar of charity,
Saint Vitus, special protector of chastity,
Saint Christophorus, mighty intercessor in dangers,
Saint Dionysius, shining mirror of faith and confidence,
Saint Cyriacus, terror of Hell,
Saint Achatius, helpful advocate in death,
Saint Eustachius, exemplar of patience in adversity,
Saint Giles, despiser of the world,
Saint Margaret, valiant champion of the Faith,
Saint Catherine, victorious defender of the Faith and of purity,
Saint Barbara, mighty patroness of the dying,

All ye Holy Helpers, et cetera
All ye Saints of God,
In temptations against faith,
In adversity and trials,
In anxiety and want,
In every combat,
In every temptation,
In sickness,
In all needs,
In fear and terror,
In dangers of salvation,
In dangers of honor,
In dangers of reputation,
In dangers of property,
In dangers by fire and water,
Be merciful, spare us, O Lord!
Be merciful, graciously hear us, O Lord!

From all sin,
deliver us, O Lord.

From Thy wrath, et cetera
From the scourge of earthquake,
From plague, famine, and war,
From lightning and storms,
From a sudden and unprovided death,
From eternal damnation,

Through the mystery of Thy holy incarnation, et cetera
Through Thy birth and Thy life,
Through Thy Cross and Passion,
Through Thy death and burial,
Through the merits of Thy blessed Mother Mary,
Through the merits of the Fourteen Holy Helpers,
On the Day of Judgment, deliver us, O Lord!

We sinners, beseech Thee hear us.
That Thou spare us,
We beseech Thee, hear us.
That Thou pardon us, et cetera
That Thou convert us to true penance,
That Thou give and preserve the fruits of the earth,
That Thou protect and propagate Thy holy Church,
That Thou preserve peace and concord among the nations,
That Thou give eternal rest to the souls of the departed,
That Thou come to our aid through the intercession of the Holy Helpers,
That through the intercession of Saint George Thou preserve us in the Faith,
That through the intercession of Saint Blase Thou confirm us in hope,
That through the intercession of Saint Erasmus Thou enkindle in us Thy holy love,
That through the intercession of Saint Pantaleon Thou give us charity for our neighbor,
That through the intercession of Saint Vitus Thou teach us the value of our soul,

That through the intercession of Saint Christophorus Thou preserve us from sin,
That through the intercession of Saint Dionysius Thou give us tranquillity of conscience,
That through the intercession of Saint Cyriacus Thou grant us resignation to Thy holy will,
That through the intercession of Saint Eustachius Thou give us patience in adversity,
That through the intercession of Saint Achatius Thou grant us a happy death,
That through the intercession of Saint Giles Thou grant us a merciful judgment,
That through the intercession of Saint Margaret Thou preserve us from Hell,
That through the intercession of Saint Catherine Thou shorten our Purgatory,
That through the intercession of Saint Barbara Thou receive us in Heaven,
That through the intercession of all the Holy Helpers Thou wilt grant our prayers,

Lamb of God, who takest away the sins of the world, spare us, O Lord.
Lamb of God, who takest away the sins of the world, graciously hear us, O Lord.
Lamb of God, who takest away the sins of the world, have mercy on us, O Lord.

V. Pray for us, ye Fourteen Holy Helpers.
R. That we may be made worthy of the promise of Christ.

Let us Pray.
—A medieval prayer

Almighty and eternal God, Who hast bestowed extraordinary graces and gifts on Thy saints George, Blase, Erasmus,

Fear and Protection

Pantaleon, Vitus, Christophorus, Dionysius, Cyriacus, Eustachius, Achatius, Giles, Margaret, Catherine, and Barbara, and hast illustrated them by miracles; we beseech Thee to graciously hear the petitions of all who invoke their intercession. Through Christ our Lord. Amen.

O God, who didst miraculously fortify the Fourteen Holy Helpers in the confession of the Faith; grant us, we beseech Thee, to imitate their fortitude in overcoming all temptations against it, and protect us through their intercession in all dangers of soul and body, so that we may serve Thee in purity of heart and chastity of body. Through Christ our Lord. Amen.

—Bible

> Even the wise man acts
> in accordance with his inner nature.
> All beings follow their nature.
> What good can repression do?
>
> Craving and aversion arise
> when the senses encounter sense-objects.
> Do not fall prey to these two
> brigands blocking your path.
>
> It is better to do your own duty
> badly, than to perfectly do
> another's; you are safe from harm
> when you do what you should be doing
>
> —Bhagavad Gita

Section Four

COMPASSION
(FORGIVENESS OF SINS)

Compassion is the cornerstone of every spiritual practice: without compassion, God would not love us. And were it not for his compassion for our human state, we would have no chance to experience his grace. In Buddhism, the practice of compassion is defined as a virtue that uproots the wish to harm others. It is an urge that makes people so sensitive to the sufferings of others that they make these sufferings their own in order to not increase them further.

Having compassion for others means to understand their shortcomings, their suffering, or even their evil, and to forgive them. It is a virtue that requires a deep understanding of the imperfection of the human condition.

Go, son, and confess, and do not abandon your habit of prayer. Know in all certainty that this temptation will be of great usefulness and consolation, and you will soon have a proof thereof.
—Saint Francis of Assisi

My greatest fault is, that after the incredible union which I have had with Thee, and which is known to Thee alone, I have not feared to sully my soul again with the same defects, which Thou has permitted to continue in me in order that I might conquer them, and thus obtain greater glory with Thee in heaven . . . permit the groans of my heart to rise even to heaven in expiation of all these faults, and of others which Thou mayest yet bring to my recollection.
—Saint Gertrude

That a reluctant person who freely and secretly discloses a secret sin in humble confession be prohibited [from serving], I esteem least of all, for fear the path of salutary confession be blocked for many who, out of certainty or suspicion of some sin, choose to keep sins totally hidden until death rather than be encouraged by this opportunity [to confess].
—Saint Anselm of Canterbury

I believe very few souls are so perfect in the beginning. We would be happy enough if they managed not to fall into these imperfections of pride. . . . God places these souls in the dark night so as to purify them of these imperfections and make them advance.
—Saint John of the Cross

Although I know well, Margaret, that because of my past wickedness I deserve to be abandoned by God, I cannot but trust in his merciful goodness. His grace has strengthened me until now and made me content to lose goods, land, and life as well, rather than to swear against my conscience. God's grace has given the king a gracious frame of mind toward me, so that as yet he has taken from me nothing but my liberty. In doing this His Majesty has done me such great good with respect to spiritual profit that I trust that among all the great benefits he has heaped so abundantly upon me I count my imprisonment the very greatest. I cannot, therefore, mistrust the grace of God.

By the merits of his bitter passion joined to mine and far surpassing in merit for me all that I can suffer myself, his bounteous goodness shall release me from the pains of purgatory and shall increase my reward in heaven besides.
—Saint Thomas More
from a letter written from prison
to his daughter Margaret

The Church teaches us that mercy belongs to God. Let us implore Him to bestow on us the spirit of mercy and compassion, so that we are filled with it and may never lose it. Only consider how much we ourselves are in need of mercy.
—Saint Vincent de Paul

Really, I am far from being a saint, and what I have just said is proof of this; instead of rejoicing, for example, at my aridity, I should attribute it to my little fervor and lack of fidelity; I should be desolate for having slept (for seven years) during my hours of prayer and my thanksgivings after Holy Communion; well, I am not desolate. I remember that little children are as pleasing to their parents when they are asleep as well as when they are wide awake; I remember, too, that when they perform operations, doctors put their patients to sleep. Finally, I remember that: "The Lord knows our weakness, that he is mindful that we are but dust and ashes."

—Saint Thérèse of Lisieux
from *Story of a Soul*

How displeasing to God are rash judgments! The judgments of the children of men are rash because they usurp the office of Our Lord, the just Judge. They are rash because the principal malice of sin depends on the intention and the counsel of the heart, and these are hidden things not known to human judges. They are rash because every person has things that could be judged, and, indeed, on which one should judge oneself.

On the cross our Savior could not entirely excuse the sin of those who crucified him, but he extenuated the malice by pleading their ignorance. When we cannot excuse a sin, let us at least make it worthy of compassion by attributing the most favorable cause we can to it, such as ignorance or weakness. We can never pass judgment on our neighbor.

—Saint Francis de Sales
from *Introduction to the Devout Life*

Repentance is the returning from the unnatural into the natural state, from the devil to God, through discipline and effort.

—Saint John of Damascus

Over and over again we are given the chance to re-examine our position—are we ready to relinquish what we have, not just to the poor to share with them what we have but to the poor who rise in revolution to take what they have been deprived of for so long? Are we ready, too, to have the drunken poor, the insane poor and what more horrible deprivation

than this, to have one's interior senses, the memory, the understanding and the will, impoverished to the extent that one is no longer rational—are we ready to be robbed in this way? Do we really welcome poverty as liberating?
—Dorothy Day

Let all bitterness and wrath and anger and clamour and railing be taken away from you, with all malice; and shew yourselves kind to one another, tender-hearted, forgiving each other, even as God also in Christ forgave you. Shew yourselves therefore initiators of God, as beloved children.
—Saint Luke
Epistle to the Ephesians

We must never dwell on our sins during prayer. Regarding our offenses, a simple humbling of our soul before God, without a thought of this offense or that, is enough . . . such thoughts act as distractions."
—Saint Jeanne de Chantal
from *Wings to the Lord*

Without hesitancy, therefore, let us love our enemies, let us do good to those who hate us, and let us pray for those who persecute us.
—Saint Augustine
the Lord's Sermon on the Mount

The life of Mary being now at its close, the most delicious music, as Saint Jerome relates, was heard in the apartment where she lay; and, according to a revelation of Saint Bridget, the room was also filled with a brilliant light. This sweet music, and the unaccustomed splendour, warned the holy Apostles that Mary was then departing. This caused them again to burst forth in tears; and raising their hands,

with one voice they exclaimed, "O, Mother, thou already goest to heaven; thou leavest us; give us thy last blessing, and never forget us miserable creatures." Mary, turning her eyes around upon all, as if to bid them a last farewell, said, "Adieu, my children; I bless you; fear not, I will never forget you."
—Saint Alphonsus de Liguori

    Lacking compassion for all beings,
    Filial piety causes Samsara.
    If one acts against the Dharma
    Friends soon turn to enemies.
    Those who only harm their friends
    Are of the devil's kin,
    However charming they may be!
—Milarepa

    The pretentious and over-critical
    Are men without compassion, faith or Bodhi-Mind
—Milarepa

Penance should be but the means to increase virtue according to the needs of the individual, and according to what the soul sees she can do in the measure of her own possibility. Otherwise, if the soul place her foundation on penance she will contaminate her own perfection, because her penance will not be done in the light of knowledge of herself and of My goodness, with discretion, and she will not seize hold of My truth; neither loving that which I love, nor hating that which I hate. This virtue of discretion is no other than a true knowledge which the soul should have of herself and of me, and in this knowledge is virtue rooted.
—Saint Catherine of Siena

Do you not know, dear daughter, that all the sufferings, which the soul endures, or can endure, in this life, are insufficient to punish one smallest fault, because the offense, being done to Me, who am the Infinite Good, calls for an infinite satisfaction? However, I wish that you should know, that not all the pains that are given to men in this life are given as punishments, but as corrections, in order to chastise a son when he offends; though it is true that both the guilt and the penalty can be expiated by the desire of the soul, that is, by true contrition, not through the finite pain endured, but through the infinite desire; because God, who is infinite, wishes for infinite love and infinite grief. Infinite grief I wish from My creature in two ways: in one way, through her sorrow for her own sins, which she has committed against Me her Creator; in the other way, through her sorrow for the sins which she sees her neighbors commit against Me. Of such as these, inasmuch as they have infinite desire, that is, are joined to Me by an affection of love, and therefore grieve when they offend Me, or see Me offended, their every pain, whether spiritual or corporeal, from wherever it may come, receives infinite merit, and satisfies for a guilt which deserved an infinite penalty, although their works are finite and done in finite time; but, inasmuch as they possess the virtue of desire, and sustain their suffering with desire, and contrition, and infinite displeasure against their guilt, their pain is held worthy. Paul explained this when he said: If I had the tongues of angels, and if I knew the things of the future and gave my body to be burned, and have not love, it would be worth nothing to me. The glorious Apostle thus shows that finite works are not valid, either as punishment or recompense, without the condiment of the affection of love.

—Saint Catherine of Siena

COMPASSION

The walls of our monasteries enclose a narrow space. To erect the structure of holiness in it, one must dig deep and build high, must descend into the depths of the dark night of one's own nothingness in order to be raised up high into the sunlight of divine love and compassion.

—Edith Stein

Section Five

POLITICS

Whether negotiating with coworkers, arguing with family members, or choosing candidates to represent our country, practicing politics nationally and socially demands our energy daily. Politics may seem irrelevant to spiritual purity, but dealing with people is an arena in which we can utilize our understanding of divine behavior. Politics tests our ability to remember and demonstrate the wisdom of the saints, namely to serve God at a time when it's much easier to simply serve oneself. Spiritual politics demands our resolve to maintain what Buddhism calls right action, right thought, and right speech. We may believe in nonviolence, for example, and be troubled by conflicting feelings when standing up for the oppressed means we are forced to support war. How we commit to the principles of divine truth is how we live our politics.

The saints, most of whom had to defend themselves against political majorities who branded them spiritual traitors or heretics, had no choice but to fight for their politics. God showed them a path that they could recognize because of their commitment to divine truth.

The more you have been tested and found worthy in dangerous company, the more you will be dear to God and God's friends.
—Saint Anselm of Canterbury

We read that useful deceit may at times be practiced... Even the Son of God pretended that he was going farther and that he did not know things which he did know, as it says in the Gospel: "Who hath touched me," and: "Where have ye laid him?" ... The goat skins were the symbol of sins, and he who clothed himself in them signifies the one who bears the sins of others.
—Saint Boniface

And because they upheld injustice in word and deed, they are punished with thorns and spikes; and since they preserved bitterness in it, they are tortured by worms; and since they were merciful to no one through any injustice, they are afflicted by the wicked spirits with fiery whips. And I saw and understood these things.
—Hildegard of Bingen

Pay no attention to the affairs of others, whether they be good or bad, for besides the danger of sin, this is a cause of distractions and lack of spirit.
—Saint John of the Cross

These beginners feel so fervent and diligent in their spiritual exercises and undertakings that a certain kind of secret pride is generated in them that begets a complacency with themselves and their accomplishments, even though holy

works do of their very nature cause humility. Then they develop a somewhat vain—at times very vain—desire to speak of spiritual things in others' presence, and sometimes even to instruct rather than be instructed; in their hearts they condemn others who do not seem to have the kind of devotion they would like them to have, and sometimes they give expression to this criticism like the Pharisee who despised the publican while he boasted and praised God for the good deeds he himself accomplished.
—Saint John of the Cross

Strive for the greater honor and glory of God in all things.
—Saint John of the Cross

Let all of us, brothers, look to the Good Shepherd Who suffered the passion of the cross to save His sheep. The sheep of the Lord followed him in tribulation and persecution, in insult and hunger, in infirmity and temptation, and in everything else, and they have received everlasting life from the Lord because of these things. Therefore, it is a great shame for us, Servants of God, that while the saints actually did such things, we wish to receive Glory and Honor by merely recounting their deeds.
—Saint Francis of Assisi

Pride can exist only in those who believe that they possess something. The fallen angel and the first man became proud and fell only because they imagined and believed that they possessed something. For neither angel nor man nor anything else has being; only one has it: God.
—Angela of Foligno

In order to avoid discord, never contradict anyone except in case of sin or some danger to a neighbor; and when neces-

sary to contradict others, do it with tact and not with temper.
— Saint Louis IX

The system is contrived, the cities are constructed, the dead carried out.
— Philip the Gnostic

And remember that all the assaults of dark and evil fortune contribute to the salvation of those who receive them with thankfulness, and are assuredly ambassadors of help.
— Saint John of Damascus

Do not imitate those persons who, after having spent a few months as a postulant or novice in a community, dress differently, even ludicrously. You are returning to the secular state. My advice is, follow the styles of the day, but from afar, as it were.
— Blessed Marie-Rose Durocher

On completing, then, the whole of what we propose in the commentaries, on which, if the Spirit will, we ministering to the urgent need, (for it is exceedingly necessary, before coming to the truth, to embrace what ought to be said by way of preface), shall address ourselves to the true Gnostic science of nature, receiving initiation into the minor mysteries before the greater; so that nothing may be in the way of the truly divine declaration of sacred things, the subjects requiring preliminary detail and statement being cleared away, and sketched beforehand. The science of nature, then, or rather observation, as contained in the Gnostic tradition according to the rule of the truth, depends on the discussion concerning cosmogony, ascending thence to the department of theology. Whence, then, we shall begin our account of what is handed down, with the creation as related by the prophets, introducing also the tenets of the heterodox, and endeavouring as far as we can to confute them. But it shall be written if God will, and as He inspires; and now we must proceed to what we proposed, and complete the discourse on ethics.

—Saint Clement of Alexandria
from *The Stromata, or Miscellany*

Beware of giving yourself to another unless first you learn to separate yourself from others. Beware also of those who flatter you with sweet words and seek to make themselves especially attractive to you by what they say, and make a show of their revelations, because these are the snares of the wicked who try to lure others after them. Beware also lest they drag you along their way.

—Angela of Foligno

Our own evil inclinations are far more dangerous than any external enemies.

—Saint Ambrose

Discretion is the only child of self-knowledge, and, wedding with charity, has indeed many other descendants, as a tree which has many branches; but that which gives life to the tree, to its branches, and its root, is the ground of humility, in which it is planted, which humility is the foster-mother and nurse of charity, by whose means this tree remains in the perpetual calm of discretion. Because otherwise the tree would not produce the virtue of discretion, or any fruit of life, if it were not planted in the virtue of humility, because humility proceeds from self-knowledge. And I have already said to you, that the root of discretion is a real knowledge of self and of my goodness, by which the soul immediately, and discreetly, renders to each one his due.

—Saint Catherine of Siena

The
Heart is right to cry

Even when the smallest drop of light,
Of love,
Is taken away.
Perhaps you may kick, moan, scream
In a dignified
Silence,

But you are so right
To do so in any fashion

Until God returns
To
You

—Hafiz

And so very many crimes are concealed; because the wicked arrange for themselves so as by all means to escape punishment.
—Saint Clement of Alexandria

You say that you are my judge, I don't know if you are [or not]; but take care not to judge wrongly, lest you place yourself in great danger; and [I] notify you of this, so that if our Lord punishes you for it, I will have done my duty in telling you.
—Saint Joan of Arc

And have no fellowship with the unfruitful works of darkness, but rather even shew them in their true nature (convict them); for the things which are done by them in secret it is a shame even to speak of. But all things when they are shewn in their true nature (convicted) by the light are made manifest; for everything that is made manifest is light.
—Saint Luke
Epistle to the Ephesians

They were like mushrooms, the best were good for nothing.
—Saint Francis de Sales

If no one ne'er accuses others,
People see one as an angel.
If one has no harmful thoughts,
Then one's merits will increase.
—Milarepa

All the trials we endure cannot be compared to these interior battles.
—Saint Teresa of Avila

It must be understood, then, that the moon derives its light from the sun; not that God was unable to grant it light of its own, but in order that rhythm and order may be unimpressed upon nature, one part ruling, the other being ruled, and that we might thus be taught to live in community and to share our possessions with one another, and to be under subjection, first to our Maker and Creator, our God and Master, and then also to the rulers set in authority over us by Him: and not to question why this man is ruler and not I myself, but to welcome all that comes from God in a gracious and reasonable spirit.

The sun and the moon, moreover, suffer eclipse, and this demonstrates the folly of those who worship the creature in place of the Creator, and teaches us how changeable and alterable all things are. For all things are changeable save God, and whatever is changeable is liable to corruption in accordance with the laws of its own nature.
—Saint John of Damascus

Whatever a great man does
ordinary people will do;

whatever standard he sets
everyone else will follow
—Bhagavad Gita

Many people cannot begin to feel the life-giving attraction for Divine Reality until they pass through the painful experiences associated with grasping at habitual enjoyment. This desperate grasping includes selfishly accumulating material wealth, arrogantly cultivating power over others, and welcoming flattery as well as enjoying absurdly refined comforts and even more bizarre diversions. We must unequivocally see through this deceptive surface in order to enter the depth of ecstatic Divine Enjoyment.
—Sri Ramakrishna

Section Six

LOVE

Virtually every saint has spoken of the pure, bright light of divine love. God is love, they say. God's love is absolute. Saint Catherine of Siena wrote extensively about God's love, calling it "a garment" and evoking the idea of love as a piece of cloth within which one is wrapped, dressed fully and in adoration of, like a new suit or dress. An individual bathing in divine love feels nothing but devotion to God. Every action and effort made is in God's name, and every experience radiates the love they feel for divinity. We all, if even for a moment, experience divine love at some point in our lives. Whether it is profound appreciation for a flower on a spring morning, or the refreshing joy of jumping into a cold lake on a hot day, that feeling of being grateful for being alive is connected to divine love.

But the Blessed of Christ never hardens the heart of the faithful. On the contrary, He softens it, as He says through the mouth of the prophet, "I will take away your heart of stone and give you a heart of flesh."
—Saint Francis of Assisi

I talk too much but I am compelled to do so by my immense love.
—Saint Anselm of Canterbury

In a similar way, since it is in harmony with the time of grace that the sacrament of union and love not only signify this union and love, but also that it be a means of inflaming the heart in that direction so as to bring about what it represents. Because what most inflames us toward mutual love and what chiefly unites the members is the oneness of the Head from whom flows a mutual affection through a stream of love that pours forth, unites and transforms; therefore this sacrament contains the true body and immaculate flesh of Christ in such a way that it pours into us, unites us to one another, and transforms us into Him through that most burning love by which He gave Himself to us, offered Himself up for us, and now returns to us and remains with us until the end of the world.
—Saint Bonaventure
on the sacrament of the Eucharist

You should have an equal love for and an equal forgetfulness of all persons, whether relatives or not, and withdraw your heart from relatives as much as from others, and in some ways even more for fear that flesh and blood might be

quickened by the natural love that is ever alive among kin, and must always be mortified for the sake of spiritual perfection.
—Saint John of the Cross

Love is the fusion of two souls in one in order to bring about mutual perfection.
—Terese of the Andes

Finally, the saint was asked whether this martyrdom of love could be put on the same level as martyrdom of the body. She answered: "We should not worry about equality. I do think, however, that the martyrdom of love cannot be relegated to a second place, for 'love is as strong as death.' For the martyrs of love suffer infinitely more in remaining in this life so as to serve God, than if they died a thousand times over in testimony to their faith and love and fidelity."
—Saint Jeanne Frances de Chantal
from the memoirs of her secretary

This thing is good and that good, but take away this and that, and regard good itself if thou canst; so wilt thou see God, not good by a good that is other than Himself, but the good of all good. For in all these good things, whether those which I have mentioned, or any else that are to be discerned or thought, we could not say that one was better than another, when we judge truly, unless a conception of the good itself had been impressed upon us, such that according to it we might both approve some things as good, and prefer one good to an other. So God is to be loved, not this and that good, but the good itself.
—Saint Augustine of Hippo

One must become mad with love in order to realize God-consciousness, which is ten million times more blissful than sexual experience.
—Sri Ramakrishna

We are born to love, we live to love, and we will die to love still more.
—Saint Joseph Cafasso

> Why Abstain?
> Why
> Abstain from love
> When like the beautiful snow goose
> Someday your soul
> Will leave this summer
> Camp?
>
> Why
> Abstain from happiness
> When like a skilled lion
> Your heart is
> Nearing
>
> And
> Will someday see
> The divine prey is
> Always
> Near!

—Hafiz

Even so ought husbands also love their own wives as being their own bodies. He that loveth his own wife loveth himself; for no one ever hated his own flesh; but nourishesth and cherisheth it.
—Saint Luke
Epistle to the Ephesians

Whatever it is which you so love that you rate it with your right eye—if it scandalizes thee—that is, if it blocks your road to true happiness, tear it out and cast it from yourself. For it is expedient for thee that one of those things should perish that thou lovest as if they were fixed members of thee, rather that thy whole body go to hell.
—Saint Augustine of Hippo
the Lord's Sermon on the Mount

I ought to die of shame to think I have not already died of gratitude to my good God.
—Saint Julie Billiart

To love God as He ought to be loved, we must be detached from all temporal love. We must love nothing but Him, or if we love anything else, we must love it only for His sake.
—Saint Peter Claver

Now love is conceived in many ways, in the form of meekness, of mildness, of patience, of liberality, of freedom from envy, of absence of hatred, of forgetfulness of injuries. In all it is incapable of being divided or distinguished: its nature is to communicate.
—Saint Clement of Alexandria

By the divine decree hollow places are made in the earth, and so into these the waters are gathered. And this is how mountains are formed. God, then, bade the first water produce living breath, since it was to be by water and the Holy Spirit that moved upon the waters in the beginning, that man was to be renewed. For this is what the divine Basilius said: Therefore it produced living creatures, small and big; whales and dragons, fish that swim in the waters, and feathered fowl. The birds form a link between water and earth and air: for they have their origin in the water, they live on the earth and they fly in the air. Water, then, is the most beautiful element and rich in usefulness, and purifies from all filth, and not only from the filth of the body but from that of the soul, if it should have received the grace of the Spirit.

—Saint John of Damascus

I remember having heard from a handmaid of God, namely, that, when she was lifted up in prayer, with great elevation of mind, God was not wont to conceal, from the eye of her intellect, the love which He had for His servants, but rather to manifest it; and, that among other things, He used to say: "Open the eye of your intellect, and gaze into Me, and you shall see the beauty of My rational creature. And look at those creatures who, among the beauties which I have given to the soul, creating her in My image and similitude, are clothed with the nuptial garment (that is, the garment of love), adorned with many virtues, by which they are united with Me through love. And yet I tell you, if you should ask Me, who these are, I should reply (said the sweet and amorous Word of God), 'they are another Myself, inasmuch as they have lost and denied their own will, and are clothed with Mine, are united to Mine, are conformed to Mine.'"

—Saint Catherine of Siena
from *On Divine Providence*

Greater love hath no man than this, that a man lay down his life for his friends.

—Bible
John 15:13

Section Seven

THE PHYSICAL BODY

Many of us are unhappy with our physical bodies. We are too tall or too short, we are not strong enough, we are always tired. Conditions of the body often break our spirit—we let the mechanics of our material selves cloud our spiritual vision, even curtail our physical growth, because we focus on them as though they are everything. The saints often had to overcome tremendous complications presented by the physical body. Many abstained from sexual activity as it distracted them from their devotion to God. Many fasted in order to keep the inner workings of the body "pure." Many battled disease and handicap. The physical body is the material home for the soul. We must care for it while we are in it. The Eastern traditions believe we will be awarded many physical forms in our long journey to eternal bliss. Whatever belief you embrace, the physical body is a part of our spiritual experience.

Have patience, for the sickness of the body is given to us by God for the salvation of our soul; for sickness is of great merit when it is endured in peace.
—Saint Francis of Assisi

The supreme power, wisdom, and benevolence of the Creator shine forth in created things insofar as the bodily senses make them known to the interior senses in the three ways. For the bodily senses serve the intellect when it investigates rationally, or believes faithfully, or contemplates intellectually. One who contemplates considers the actual existence of things; one who believes considers the habitual course of things; and one who investigates with reason considers the potential excellence of things.
—Saint Bonaventure

Man, too, is God's handiwork, like every other creature. But man is also God's journeyman and the foreshadowing of the mysteries of God.
—Hildegard of Bingen

The soul, dwelling in the body of frail humanity, is darkened in the same manner as a person who stands in a narrow space, and is surrounded on all sides by a vapour exhaling from a cooking vessel. And when the body is afflicted by any evil, the part which suffers is to the soul as a beam from the sun which enlightens the air, and from which it receives marvelous clearness; therefore the heavier one's sufferings are, the purer is the light the soul receives.
—Saint Gertrude

For the torments of these punishments purge the souls, who, living in the transitory world deserved there the purgation of their sins through punishment in the nontransitory [world]. They were not fully purged in the flesh, having been prevented by death, or even tried in the world by divine flails of compassionate God. Therefore they will be purged by these punishments, unless they are snatched from them by the labors of men and the virtues of the saints, which God worked in them through the invocation of the piety of divine grace.
—Hildegard of Bingen

For I trust, in whatever manner I die, that I shall not be deprived of the mercy of my God, without which my eternal ruin would be inevitable, whether I die an unprepared death, or whether I have long anticipated my end.
—Saint Gertrude

O soul pressed down by the corruptible body, and weighed down by earthly thoughts, many and various; behold and see, if thou canst, that God is truth.
—Saint Augustine of Hippo

Well, the body tills the ground, and hastes to it; but the soul is raised to God: trained in the true philosophy, it speeds to its kindred above, turning away from the lusts of the body, and besides these, from toil and fear, although we have shown that patience and fear belong to the good man.
—Saint Clement of Alexandria

Under its burden body, soul and spirit lose their strength and health, their clarity and beauty. Just as it is scarcely possible for one impaired by original sin to own things without clinging to them, so there is also the danger that any natural affection may degenerate into passion with all of its devastating consequences.

—Edith Stein

> Removing the Shoe from the Temple
> Once someone asked me,
> "Why do saints seek divine annihilation
> And are often humble
> And like to spend their free time
> Upon their knees?"
>
> I replied,
>
> "It is a matter of etiquette."
>
> Then they said,
>
> "What do you mean, Hafiz?"
>
> "Well," I continued,
> "When one goes into a mosque or temple
> Is it not common to remove what
> Covers your
> Feet?
>
> So too does it happen
> With this whole mind and body—
> That is something like a shoe sole—
> When one begins to realize
> Upon Whom you are really standing,
>
> One begins
> To remove the "shoe" from the
> "Temple"
>
> —Hafiz

On those who do not do penance

See, blind ones, deceived by your enemies: by the flesh,

the world, and the devil; since it is sweet to the body to work sin and bitter to work to serve God; since all vices and sins come forth and proceed from the heart of man, just as the Lord says in the Gospel (cf. Mk 7:21). And you will have nothing in this age nor in the one to come. And you think you will possess the vanities of this age for a long time, but you are deceived, since there will come the day and hour, of which you do not think, know or pay attention; the body weakens, death approaches and so one dies a bitter death. And wheresoever, whensoever, howsoever a man dies in culpable sin without penance and satisfaction, if he can make satisfaction and does not, the devil tears his soul from his body with such anguish and tribulation, that no one can know it, except him who experiences it. And all talents and power and knowledge and wisdom (2 Chron 1:12), which they thought they had, and he bears it away from them (cf. Lk 8:18; Mk 4:25).

—Saint Francis of Assisi
Letter to the Faithful

As to my dress, since I bear it by command of God and for His service, I do not think I have done wrong at all; so soon as it shall please God to prescribe it, I will take it off.

—Saint Joan of Arc

Wherein aforetime ye walked according to the prince of the power of the air, of the spirit, that now worketh in the sons of disobedience; among whom we also all once lived in the lusts of our flesh, doing the will of the flesh and of the mind and were children by nature of wrath, even as the rest of men; But god, being rich of mercy, for His great love wherewith He loved us, even when we were dead through our trespasses quickened us together with the Christ (by grace

have ye been saved), and raised us up with Him and made us sit with Him in the heavenly order in Christ Jesus.
—Saint Luke
Epistle to the Ephesians

Human nature grows tired of always doing the same thing, and it is God's will that this because of the opportunity of practicing two great virtues. The first is perseverance, which will bring us to our goal. The other is steadfastness, which overcomes the difficulties on the way.
—Saint Vincent de Paul

Listen, great pandit Naropa:
Until you understand that (all)
Appearance due to interdependent factors has never come about,
Do not fail
To accumulate merit and knowledge, which are like the two wheels of a carriage.

Towards the teacher who points out the unoriginated
Let appearance rising red and white, and the capacity
For thought, fly like a crow from off a ship.
Enjoy the goods of earth, Naropa.
—Tilopa
to his disciple, Naropa

Oh Faithful patrons and disciples,
Evildoers are many, but virtue practicers are few.
All sufferings are of sins the retribution,
All joys of virtues are the meed,
Yet both are due to all that one has done.

Let us now make a vow to meet
Again and again in future times!
—Milarepa

Accordingly the everlasting God generates His own Word which is perfect, without beginning and without end, that God, Whose nature and existence are above time, may not engender in time. But with man clearly it is otherwise, for generation is with him a matter of sex, and destruction and flux and increase and body clothe him round about, and he possesses a nature which is male or female. For the male requires the assistance of the female. But may He Who surpasses all, and transcends all thought and comprehension, be gracious to us.
—Saint John of Damascus

See my children, I often think that we are like those little heaps of sand that the wind raises on the road, which whirl round for a moment, and are scattered directly. . . . We have brothers and sisters who are dead. Well, they are reduced to that little handful of dust of which I was speaking. Worldly people say, it is too difficult to save one's soul. Yet nothing is easier. To observe the Commandments of God and the Church, and to avoid the seven capital sins; or if you like to put it so, to do good and avoid evil: that is all.
—Saint John Mary Vianney

Love is the first ingredient in the relief of suffering.
—Padre Pio

What beauty? I don't see my beauty at all; I see only the graces I've received from God. You always misunderstand me; you don't know, then, that I'm only a little seedling, a little almond.
—Saint Thérèse of Lisieux

Sometimes I felt such great love it seemed I could not go on living if these desires continued any longer. . . . Once when the violence of love took hold of me, I grasped a needle and on my chest drew these letters: J.A.M., which means Jesus My Love.

—Terese of the Andes

Our Lord and Savior lifted up his voice and said with incomparable majesty: "Let all men know that grace comes after tribulation. Let them know that without the burden of afflictions it is impossible to reach the height of grace. Let them know that the gifts of grace increase as the struggles increase. Let men take care not to stray and be deceived. This is the only true stairway to paradise, and without the cross they can find no road to climb to heaven."

When I heard these words, a strong force came upon me and seemed to place me in the middle of a street, so that I might say in a loud voice to people of every age, sex and status: "Hear, O people; hear, O nations. I am warning you about the commandment of Christ by using words that came from his own lips: 'We cannot obtain grace unless we suffer afflictions.' We must heap trouble upon trouble to attain a deep participation in the divine nature, the glory of the sons of God and perfect happiness of soul."

If only mortals would learn how great it is to possess divine grace, how beautiful, how noble, how precious. How many riches it hides within itself, how many joys and delights! No one would complain about his cross or about troubles that may happen to him, if he would come to know the scales on which they are weighed when they are distributed to men.

—Saint Rose of Lima

> We do not get a human life
> Just for the asking.
> Birth in a human body

Is the reward for good deeds
In former births.
Life waxes and wanes imperceptibly,
It does not stay long.
The leaf that has once fallen
Does not return to the branch.
Behold the Ocean of Transmigration.
With its swift, irresistible tide.
O Lal Giridhara, O pilot of my soul,
Swiftly conduct my barque to the further shore.
Mira is the slave of Lal Giridhara.
She says: Life lasts but a few days only.

Life in the world is short,
Why shoulder an unnecessary load
Of worldly relationships?
Thy parents gave thee birth in the world,
But the Lord ordained thy fate.
Life passes in getting and spending,
No merit is earned by virtuous deeds.
I will sing the praises of Hari
In the company of the holy men,
Nothing else concerns me.
Mira's Lord is the courtly Giridhara,
She says: Only by Thy power
Have I crossed to the further shore.

—Mira Bai

If we are, in fact, now occupied in good deeds, we should not attribute the strength with which we are doing them to ourselves. We must not count on ourselves, because even if we know what kind of person we are today, we do not know what we will be tomorrow. Nobody must rejoice in the security of their own good deeds. As long as we are still

experiencing the uncertainties of this life, we do not know what end may follow . . . we must not trust in our own virtues.
—Saint Gregory the Great
from *Be Friends of God*

The fruit which I destine for them, constrained by the prayers of My servants, is that I give them light, and that I wake up in them the hound of conscience, and make them smell the odor of virtue, and take delight in the conversation of My servants. Sometimes I allow the world to show them what it is, so that, feeling its diverse and various passions, they may know how little stability it has, and may come to lift their desire beyond it, and seek their native country, which is the Eternal Life. And so I draw them by these, and by many other ways, for the eye cannot see, nor the tongue relate, nor the heart think, how many are the roads and ways which I use, through love alone, to lead them back to grace, so that My truth may be fulfilled in them. I am constrained to do so by that inestimable love of Mine, by which I created them, and by the love, desire, and grief of My servants, since I am no despiser of their tears, and sweat, and humble prayers; rather I accept them, inasmuch as I am He who give them this love for the good of souls and grief for their loss.
—Saint Catherine of Siena
from *On Divine Providence*

Do any actions you must do
since action is better than inaction;
even the existence of your body
depends on necessary actions.

The whole world becomes a slave
to its own activity, Arjuna;

if you want to be truly free
perform all actions as worship.
—Bhagavad Gita

Don't be upset about those outbursts, although you should never be satisfied with them. If the Lord doesn't give you the grace of inexhaustible and continual gentleness, it is in order to leave you a means to practise holy humility. As a penance, every time you let yourself go, you must show yourself twice as gentle immediately.
—Padre Pio

Be conscious, O man, of the wondrous state in which the Lord God has placed you, for He created you and formed you to the image of His beloved Son according to the body, and to His likeness according to the spirit. And yet all the creatures under heaven each according to its nature serve, know, and obey their Creator better than you. And even the demons did not crucify him, but you together with them have crucified Him and crucify Him even now by delighting in vices and sins.
—Saint Francis of Assisi

Section Eight

SERVICE

The saints lived their lives in service to God. Whether his or her mission was to interpret scripture, build monasteries, or care for the sick, each saint gave himself or herself over completely to work, or service, to God. And we can learn from their examples and perhaps dedicate even a small part of our busy lives to serving others. We might volunteer to feed the homeless, or to coach a neighborhood youth sports team. Service may also be a matter of dedicating one's daily work—even if it's in a corporate environment—to a higher cause.

I have resolved in my heart to abandon the world and follow you in that which you command.
—Saint Francis of Assisi

Let us, therefore, be monks together, let us serve God together, so that we may rejoice together over each other now and in the future. We are one flesh and one blood; let us be one soul and one spirit.
—Saint Anselm of Canterbury

But afflictions and trials of the heart in humility, patience, and other virtues impart the greatest luster to the soul, as they touch it more keenly, efficaciously, and intimately; works of charity, above all, give it an admirable serenity and brightness.
—Saint Gertrude

But there are scarcely any beginners who at the time of their initial fervor do not fall victim to some of these imperfections. But souls who are advancing in perfection at this time act in an entirely different manner and with a different quality of spirit. They receive great benefit from their humility, by which they not only place little importance on their deeds, but also take very little self-satisfaction from them. They think everyone else is far better than they are, and usually possess a holy envy of them and would like to emulate their service of God.
—Saint John of the Cross

They very generously give all they have. Their pleasure is to know how to live for love of God or neighbor without

these spiritual or temporal things. As I say, they set their eyes on the substance of interior perfection, on pleasing God and not themselves.
—Saint John of the Cross

The sublime and ineffable state of samadhi, total absorption in Divine Presence, is reached most directly and naturally through selfless love.
—Sri Ramakrishna

And he who does any duty for the sake of recompense, is he not held fast in the custom of the world, either as one who has done well, hastening to receive a reward, or as an evildoer avoiding retribution? We must, as far as we can, imitate the Lord. And he will do so, who complies with the will of God, receiving freely, giving freely, and receiving as a worthy reward the citizenship itself. "The hire of an harlot shall not come into the sanctuary," it is said: accordingly it was forbidden to bring to the altar the price of a dog.
—Saint Clement of Alexandria

The Lord measures our perfection neither by the multitude nor the magnitude of our deeds, but by the manner in which we perform them.
—Saint John of the Cross

I did not come to be served but to serve, says the Lord. Those who are placed over others should glory in such an office only as much as they would were they assigned the task of washing the feet of the brothers. And the more they are upset about their office being taken from them than they would be over the loss of the office of (washing) feet, so much the more do they store up treasures to the peril of their souls.
—Saint Francis of Assisi

The prophet, who serves the Lord in complete purity of heart and completely stripped of everything earthly, is also a model of obedience. He stands before God's face like the angels before the eternal throne, awaiting his sign, always ready to serve. He has no other will than the will of his Lord. When God bids, he goes before the king and fearlessly risks giving him bad news that must arouse his hatred. When God wills it, he leaves the country at the threat of violence; but he also returns at God's command, though the danger has not disappeared. Anyone who is so unconditionally faithful to God can also be certain of God's faithfulness.
—Edith Stein

Lord, make me an instrument of your peace,
  Where there is hatred, let me sow love;
  . . . where there is injury, pardon;
  . . . where there is doubt, faith;
  . . . where there is despair, hope;
  . . . where there is darkness, light;
  . . . where there is sadness, joy;

O Divine Master, grant that I may not so much seek
  . . . to be consoled as to console;
  . . . to be understood as to understand;
  . . . to be loved as to love.

For it is in giving that we receive;
  . . . it is in pardoning that we are pardoned;
  . . . and it is in dying that we are born to eternal life.
—Prayer of Saint Francis of Assisi

For mental prayer in my opinion is nothing else than an intimate sharing between friends; it means taking time frequently to be alone with him who we know loves us.
—Saint Teresa of Avila

Our greatest fault is that we wish to serve God in our way, not in His way—according to our will, not according to His will. When He wishes us to be sick, we wish to be well; when He desires us to serve Him by sufferings, we desire to serve Him by works; when He wishes us to exercise charity, we wish to exercise humility; when He seeks from us resignation, we wish for devotion, a spirit of prayer or some other virtue. And this is not because the things we desire may be more pleasing to Him, but because they are more to our taste. This is certainly the greatest obstacle we can raise to our own perfection, for it is beyond doubt that if we were to wish to be Saints according to our own will, we shall never be so at all. To be truly a Saint, it is necessary to be one according to the will of God.
—Saint Francis de Sales

Our Lord needs from us neither great deeds nor profound thoughts. Neither intelligence nor talents. He cherishes simplicity.
—Saint Thérèse of Lisieux

Oh my Lord! How true it is that whoever works for you is paid in troubles! And what a precious price to those who love you if we understand its value.
—Saint Teresa of Avila

I came to the Irish people to preach the Gospel and endure the taunts of unbelievers, putting up with reproaches about my earthly pilgrimage, suffering many persecutions, even bondage, and losing my birthright of freedom for the benefit of others.

If I am worthy, I am ready also to give up my life, without hesitation and most willingly, for Christ's name. I want to spend myself for that country, even in death, if the Lord should grant me this favor.

It is among that people that I want to wait for the promise made by him, who assuredly never tells a lie. He makes this promise in the Gospel: 'They shall come from the east and west and sit down with Abraham, Isaac and Jacob.' This is our faith: believers are to come from the whole world.

—Saint Patrick

His motto: "Labor without stopping. Do all the good works you can while you still have the time."

—John of God

WHEN God created the world He commanded each tree to bear fruit after its kind; and even so He bids Christians—the living trees of His Church—to bring forth fruits of devotion, each one according to his kind and vocation. A different exercise of devotion is required of each—the noble, the artisan, the servant, the prince, the maiden and the wife; and furthermore such practice must be modified according to the strength, the calling, and the duties of each individual.

—Saint Francis de Sales

So many poor people come here that I very often wonder how we can care for them all, but Jesus Christ provides all things and nourishes everyone. Many of them come to the house of God, because the city of Granada is large and very cold, especially now in winter. More than a hundred and ten are now living here, sick and healthy, servants and pilgrims. Since this house is open to everyone, it receives the sick of every type and condition: the crippled, the disabled, lepers, mutes, the insane, paralytics, those suffering from scurvy and those bearing the afflictions of old age, many children, and above all countless pilgrims and travelers, who come here, and for whom we furnish the fire, water, and salt, as well as the utensils to cook their food. And for all of this no payment is requested, yet Christ provides.

I work here on borrowed money, a prisoner for the sake of Jesus Christ. And often my debts are so pressing that I dare not go out of the house for fear of being seized by my creditors. Whenever I see so many poor brothers and neighbors of mine suffering beyond their strength and overwhelmed with so many physical or mental ills which I cannot alleviate, then I become exceedingly sorrowful; but I trust in Christ, who knows my heart. And so I say, "Woe to the man who trusts in men rather than in Christ."

—Saint John of God
from a letter

A stage of the journey has been accomplished. Let us not stop along the road, let us readily answer God's call for the good cause, each one of us fulfilling our duties: I with the incessant prayer of a useless servant of our Lord Jesus Christ and you with the ardent desire of clasping all suffering humanity to your hearts to present it with me to the mercy of the Heavenly Father. Go ahead then with humility of spirit and your hearts on high.

—Padre Pio

Some sages say that all action
is tainted and should be relinquished;
others permit only acts
of worship, control and charity.

Here is the truth: these acts
of worship, control and charity
purify the heart and therefore
should not be relinquished but performed

But even the most praiseworthy acts
should be done with complete nonattachment

and with no concern for results;
this is my final judgement.

—Bhagavad Gita

If it is thy wish to found a convent in this town, in which thou mayest serve God according to thy heart's desires, I will help thee most willingly, for the salvation of my soul.

—Saint Francis of Assisi

Find a Better Job

>Now
>That
>All your worry
>Has proved such an
>Unlucrative
>Business,
>Why
>Not
>Find a better
>Job

—Hafiz

Section Nine

INDECISION

While there is nothing inherently wrong with asking questions, the inability to decide on the correct answers can make us unhappy. If we never decide on issues of faith, we remain uncommitted, uncertain, and on the edge of a relationship with God. In the material world, indecision is much the same: We don't progress with people whom we can't decide if we love, with a career we're not certain is right for us, with a community that we're not sure we like all the time. Indecision can even make us lonely.

Therefore, O soul, make a daily examination of your life. Look carefully to see how far you have advanced and how much further you have yet to go; look at the quality of your morals and the character of your love; examine to what degree you are like God and to what degree you are unlike God; take note of how close to God, or how far removed from God you are. Remember this always: it is better and more praiseworthy to know yourself than to ignore yourself while you come to know the course of the stars, the power of herbs, the structure of human nature, and the nature of animals—in short, all other things of heaven and earth. Turn to your inner self, if not always, then at least from time to time. Master your affections, guide your actions, correct your ways.
—Saint Bonaventure

We should take care not to follow our own will excessively against all other advice, even if it appears to us to be right. For what appears right to a single person may not be right, since it is written; The way of the fool is right in his own eyes.
—Saint Anselm of Canterbury

They maintain a weak intention towards the good works when they ought to advance bravely in deeds of righteousness and they do not run single-mindedly in the teachings of the Church because their minds concentrate on earthly rather than heavenly matters; and therefore they are foolish before God, because they wish to understand by secular wisdom what cannot be comprehended.
—Hildegard of Bingen

I see in heaven a house of marvelous fairness and greatness. And in that house was a pulpit and in the pulpit a Book. And I see two standing before the pulpit; that is to say, an angel and the fiend.
—Saint Birgitta

They are often extremely anxious that God remove their faults and imperfections, but their motive is personal peace rather than God. They fail to realize that were God to remove their faults they might very well become more proud and presumptuous. They dislike praising anyone else, but they love to receive praise, and sometimes they even seek it. In this they resemble the foolish virgins who had to seek oil from others when their own lamps were extinguished.
—Saint John of the Cross

In a letter to a devotee:
But the real reason that you do not meditate well is, I think that you approach meditation in an altered state, coupled with a great anxiety to find something with which to console your spirit—and that is sufficient not to allow you to find what you are looking for and to be unable to bring your mind into the meditation of truth and your heart empty of affections. Daughter of mine, be aware that when one seeks with great hurry and avidity something lost, one will touch it, one will see it a hundred times and yet will never notice it. From this vain and useless anxiety you can derive nothing but a great tiredness of spirit and a blurred mind. I only know of the following remedy: come out of this anxiety, because it is the worst traitor that real virtue and devotion could ever have; it feigns to work well, but it does not—it only slows us and does not let us run in order for us to fall down.
—Padre Pio

A little drop of simple obedience is worth a million times more than a whole vase of the choicest contemplation.
—Saint Mary Magdalen de' Pazzi

The most deadly poison of our times is indifference.... And this happens, although the praise of God should know no limits.... Let us strive, therefore, to praise Him to the greatest extent of our powers.
—Saint Maximilian Kolbe

ANXIETY of mind is not so much an abstract temptation, as the source whence various temptations arise. Sadness, when defined, is the mental grief we feel because of our involuntary ailments; —whether the evil be exterior, such as poverty, sickness or contempt; or interior, such as ignorance, dryness, depression or temptation. Directly that the soul is conscious of some such trouble, it is downcast, and so trouble sets in. Then we at once begin to try to get rid of it, and find means to shake it off; and so far rightly enough, for it is natural to us all to desire good, and shun that which we hold to be evil.
—Saint Francis de Sales
#316 from *Introduction to the Devout Life*

About Jesus Christ and the Church, I simply know they're just one thing, and we shouldn't complicate the matter.
—Saint Joan of Arc
as recorded at her trial

If anyone strives to be delivered from his troubles out of love of God, he will strive patiently, gently, humbly and calmly, looking for deliverance rather to God's Goodness and Providence than to his own industry or efforts; but if self-love is the prevailing object, he will grow hot and eager in seeking relief, as though all depended more upon him-

self than upon God. I do not say that the person thinks so, but he acts eagerly as though he did think it. Then if he does not find what he wants at once, he becomes exceedingly impatient and troubled, which does not mend matters, but on the contrary makes them worse, and so he gets into an unreasonable state of anxiety and distress, till he begins to fancy that there is no cure for his trouble. Thus you see how a disturbance, which was right at the outset, begets anxiety, and anxiety goes on into an excessive distress, which is exceedingly dangerous.
—Saint Francis de Sales

> He who controls his mind
> and has cut off desire and anger
> realizes the Self; he knows
> that God's bliss is nearer than near.
>
> Closing his eyes, his vision
> focused between the eyebrows,
> making the in-breath and the out-breath
> equal as they pass through his nostrils,
>
> he controls his sense and his mind,
> intent upon liberation;
> when desire, fear, and anger have left him,
> that man is forever free.
> —Bhagavad Gita

If You Don't Stop That

> I used to live in
> A cramped house with confusion
> And pain
>
> But then I met the Friend
> And started getting drunk

INDECISION

And singing all
Night

Confusion and pain
Started acting nasty,
Making threats,
With talk like this,

"If you don't stop 'that'—
All that fun—

We're
Leaving."
—Hafiz

When paradise is poured into a heart, this afflicted, exiled, weak and mortal heart cannot bear it without weeping.
—Padre Pio

This unresting anxiety is the greatest evil which can happen to the soul, sin only excepted. Just as internal commotions and seditions ruin a commonwealth, and make it incapable of resisting its foreign enemies, so if our heart be disturbed and anxious, it loses power to retain such graces as it has, as well as strength to resist the temptations of the Evil One, who is all the more ready to fish (according to an old proverb) in troubled waters.
—Saint Francis de Sales

To do wrong, then, is not good, for no one does wrong except for some other thing; and nothing that is necessary is voluntary. To do wrong, then, is voluntary, so that it is not necessary. But the good differ especially from the bad in inclinations and good desires. For all depravity of soul is accompanied with want of restraint; and he who acts from passion, acts from want of restraint and from depravity.
—Saint Clement of Alexandria

Section Ten

DISEASE/HEALING

We have never been more interested in the art of healing than we are now. We know the benefits of healing our bodies from stress, our minds from past psychological trauma. Healing products and practices are everywhere; herbal remedies, meditation training, and martial arts have become popular among millions who want to relieve stress and live happy lives. The saints insist that in our weaknesses we can find strength. They suggest that we look within to find a source of divine love and help in healing.

The highest gift and grace of the Holy Spirit that Christ concedes to His friends is to conquer oneself and, out of love of Christ, to endure willingly sufferings, injuries, insults, and discomfort. We cannot glory in all the other gifts of God because they are not ours but they are of God, because of which the Apostle says, "What do you have that does not come from God? If you have had it from God, why do you glory in it as if it were your own?"
—Saint Francis of Assisi

When I am weak, then I am strong.
—Saint Paul

If any baby lying in its cradle is suffused and vexed with blood between the skin and the flesh so that it is greatly troubled, take new and recent leaves from the aspen and put them on a simple linen cloth and put him down to sleep, wrapping him up so that he will sweat and extract the virtue from the leaves; and he will get well.
—Hildegard of Bingen

For the deeper that I was in sin, the more grievously am I gone down into pain. And therefore whatever is done to the praise of God for me, it lifts me up from pain; and specially that prayer and good that is done by rightful men and the friends of God and benefits that are done by well-gotten goods and deeds of charity. Such things, truly, they were that make me each day become closer to God.
—Saint Birgitta

But people should insofar as possible strive to do their part in purifying and perfecting themselves and thereby merit God's divine cure. In this cure God will heal them of what through their own efforts they were unable to remedy. No matter how much individuals do through their own efforts, they cannot actively purify themselves enough to be disposed in the least degree for the divine union of the perfection of love. God must take over and purge them in that fire that is dark for them.
—Saint John of the Cross

Do you hear the groans of the wounded on the battlefields in the west and the east? You are not a physician and not a nurse and cannot bind up the wounds. You are enclosed in a cell and cannot get to them. Do you hear the anguish of the dying? You would like to be a priest and comfort them. Does the lament of the widows and orphans distress you? You would like to be an angel of mercy and help them. Look at the Crucified. If you are nuptially bound to him by the faithful observance of your holy vows, *your being* is precious blood. Bound to him, you are omnipresent as he is. You cannot help here or there like the physician, the nurse, the priest. You can be at all fronts, wherever there is grief, in the power of the cross. Your compassionate love takes you everywhere, this love from the divine heart. Its precious blood is poured everywhere soothing, healing, saving.
—Edith Stein

If a man is to enter this Divine union, all that lives in his soul must die, both little and much, small and great, and that the soul must be without desire for all this, and detached from it, even as though it existed not for the soul, neither the soul for it.
—Saint John of the Cross

A voluntary death, when it is chosen upon such an authority, is very honorable, so if any man takes away his own life without the approbation of the priests and the Senate, they give him none of the honors of a decent funeral, but throw his body into a ditch.

—Saint Thomas More

> Every part of you has a secret language.
> Your hands and your feet say what you've done
> And every need brings in what's needed
> Pain bears its cure like a child
>
> —Rumi

Prayer for the Sick

Watch, O Lord, with those who wake, or watch, or weep tonight, and give your angels charge over those who sleep.

Tend your sick ones, O Lord Christ.
Rest your weary ones.
Bless your dying ones.
Soothe your suffering ones.
Pity your afflicted ones.
Shield your joyous ones.
And for all your love's sake. Amen.

—Saint Augustine

Prayer is an act of love, words are not needed. Even if sickness distracts from thoughts, all that is needed is the will to love.

—Saint Teresa of Avila

Let the body endure its inevitable ailments, but you, O

mind, be immersed in the Divine Nature and enjoy unalloyed bliss.
—Sri Ramakrishna

A single word from him—a look, a smile, his very presence—sufficed to dispel melancholy, drive away temptation and produce holy resolution in the soul.
—Saint John Bosco
writing about Saint Joseph

There is no such thing as bad weather. All weather is good because it is God's.
—Saint Teresa of Avila

Elegance

It
Is not easy
To stop thinking ill
Of others.

Usually one must enter into a friendship
With a person

Who has accomplished that great feat himself.
Then

Something
Might start to rub off on you
Of that

True
Elegance.
—Hafiz

Love our Lady, make others love her. Always say your Rosary and say it well. Satan always tries to destroy this prayer, but he will never succeed. It is the prayer of her who triumphs over everything and everyone.

—Padre Pio

How can I write a letter? When I am unable to write? I can not speak any thing, when I want to say some thing, my eyes get flooded with tears. As I hold up the pen, my hand trembles, and my heart puzzles. How can I hold up Thy lotus feet! When I can't stand even, as my entire body staggers! Mira begs from her Lord Krishna, keep a place for her, under Thy lotus feet!

—Mira Bai

[The soul is] simple, invisible, incorporeal, not divided into parts like the body, present as a whole in whatever she does . . . the soul is not in a particular place. . . . As God is everywhere . . . so the soul is everywhere in the body, more powerfully in heart and brain, as one says that God is in a special way in heaven. . . .

—Saint Alphais

Grains of wheat, when ground in the mill, turn into flour. With this flour we make the wafer of the holy Eucharist. Grapes, when crushed in the wine press, yield their juice. This juice turns into wine. Similarly, suffering so crushes us that we turn into better human beings.

—Blessed Alphonsa of India

Think well. Speak well. Do well. These three things, through the mercy of God, will make a man go to Heaven.

—Saint Camillus de Lellis

Everything comes from love, all is ordained for the salvation of man, God does nothing without this goal in mind.

—Saint Catherine of Siena

Make a little cell in your heart for Jesus of the Agony; take refuge there, when you hear Him outraged by men, try to make reparation; you, at least, love Him and keep your heart quite pure for Him. Oh! If you only knew how the good God loves pure hearts! It is there that He loves to reign.
—Saint Elizabeth of the Trinity

O Lord, we bring before you the distress and dangers of peoples and nations, the pleas of the imprisoned and the captive, the sorrows of the grief-stricken, the needs of the refugee, the impotence of the weak, the weariness of the despondent, and the diminishments of the aging. O Lord, stay close to all of them. Amen.
—Saint Anselm of Canterbury

We are like children, who stand in need of masters to enlighten us and direct us; and God has provided for this, by appointing his angels to be our teachers and guides.
—Saint Thomas Aquinas

The angel's nature then is rational, and intelligent, and endowed with free-will, change, able in will, or fickle. For all that is created is changeable, and only that which is uncreated is unchangeable. Also all that is rational is endowed with free-will. As it is, then, rational and intelligent, it is endowed with free-will: and as it is created, it is changeable, having power either to abide or progress in goodness, or to turn towards evil.
—Saint John of Damascus

About beings, know that they die;
about gods, know the Supreme
Person; and know that true worship
is I myself, here, in this body.

Whoever in his final moments
thinks of me only, is sure
to enter my state of being
once his body is dead.

Whatever the state of being
that a man may focus upon
at the end, when he leaves his body,
to that state of being he will go.
—Bhagavad Gita

And again I saw Him praying in me, and I was as it were within my body, and I heard Him above me, that is, over the inward man, and there He prayed mightily with groanings. And all the time I was astonished, and wondered, and thought with myself who it could be that prayed in me. But at the end of the prayer He spoke, saying that He was the Spirit; and so I woke up, and remembered the Apostle saying: The Spirit helpeth the infirmities of our prayer. For we know not what we should pray for as we ought; but the Spirit Himself asketh for us with unspeakable groanings, which cannot be expressed in words; and again: The Lord our advocate asketh for us.

—Saint Patrick
from *The Confessions*

Section Eleven

EDUCATION

According to the *Catholic Encyclopedia*, education includes all those experiences by which intelligence is developed, knowledge acquired, and character formed. In a narrower sense, it is the work done by certain agencies and institutions, the home and the school, for the express purpose of training immature minds. Many of the saints were great thinkers and educators who knew well the value of learning. Saint Thomas Aquinas, Saint Augustine of Hippo, and Saint Catherine of Siena were great intellectuals on the subjects of God, the church, and society, and they all flourished in their service as saints in part because of their higher levels of education. They worked within formal educational institutions, while Saint Francis, Ramakrishna and others developed their most profound intelligence outside of institutions through direct experience and divine epiphany. Education, to all saints, is a state of mind, one in which the individual remains open to and discerning of all teachings and teachers, which can appear in many forms.

O Brother Leo, little lamb of God, although the Friar Minor might speak with the tongue of an angel and know the course of the heavens and the virtues of herbs, and if all the treasures of the earth were revealed to him and he were to know all the properties of birds and of fishes and of all men and animals and of trees and stones and roots and waters, write down that in that there is no perfect joy.
—Saint Francis of Assisi

The teacher and guide who hides the sins of the people in silence becomes thereby guilty of the blood of lost souls.
—Saint Boniface

O king of all glory and bliss, giver of all wisdom and granter of all virtues, why do you choose me for such work, who has wasted my body in sins? I am like a donkey, unlearned and unwise and defective in virtues; and I have trespassed in all things and amended nothing.

Lord Jesus Christ answered: if money or other metal were presented to a lord, who should marvel, though he made of it for himself crowns or rings or coins to his own profit. So it is no marvel though I receive the hearts of my friends presented to me and do my will with them. And just as much as one has less understanding and another more, so do I use the conscience of each as is expedient to my praise. For the heart of a rightful man is my money; therefore be firm and ready to do my will.
—Saint Birgitta

The teacher is to live so justly that his deeds shall not contradict his words and that, while he himself may live pru-

dently, he shall not be silently condemned for the sins of others. He is set over the Church of God to this end, that he not only may set an example of right living to others, but, through his dutiful preaching, may bring every man's sins before his eyes and show him what punishment awaits the hard of heart and what rewards the obedient.
—Saint Boniface

For I would prefer part of an obscure and unusual work faithfully copied than the whole of it corrupted by mistakes.
—Saint Anselm of Canterbury

There is more value in a little study of humility and in a single act of it than in all the knowledge in the world.
—Saint Teresa of Avila

Those who do not know how, let them learn, not on account of the cupidity to receive a price for work, but on account of the example it gives to repel idleness.
—Saint Francis of Assisi

In order to come to union with the wisdom of God, the soul has to proceed rather by unknowing than by knowing. . . .
—Saint John of the Cross

Man's estrangement from God means that he must struggle to attain knowledge. Because struggle is mandated, the opacity of signs, the obscurity of symbols, the ambiguity of language, and the figurative meaning of texts are logical necessities. They are the scaffolding that the active learner must climb to participate in universal and divine knowledge. Finally, through the resolution of obscurity, the learner becomes deeply involved with and personally committed to the divine meanings as they are encountered.
—Saint Augustine of Hippo

On his efforts in writing:
> Lady Gentleness seems to be making progress in me, but I myself am not satisfied on this point. However I don't want to lose heart. I have made many promises, dear Father, to Jesus and Mary. I want to acquire this virtue with their help and in return, as well as keeping the other promises. I have also promised to make this the subject of constant meditation and to suggest it continually to others also.
> —Padre Pio

The Lord said to Adam: eat of every tree; do not eat of the tree of knowledge of good and evil. He was able to eat of every tree of paradise since he did not sin as long as he did not go against obedience. For the person eats of the tree of the knowledge of good who appropriates to himself his own will and thus exalts himself over the good things which the Lord says and does in him; and thus, through the suggestions of the devil and the transgression of the command, what he eats becomes for him the fruit of the knowledge of evil. Therefore, it is necessary that he bear the punishment.
—Saint Francis of Assisi

No results of genuine and lasting spiritual value will be achieved by mere lectures, regardless of how well intentioned they may be. The fire of realization is necessary to ignite hearts.
—Sri Ramakrishna

Education is not confused as it is in this country, where pupils are taught to reverence God and Country, where they are taught to take God into partnership in order to prosper. And if anything is more than utter atheism, it is this attempt to equate God and country, and to make God serve our own purposes. We all do it, we are all guilty. And we need to remind ourselves that the reason for man's existence is to love, honor and serve God.

—Dorothy Day

The soul cannot have true knowledge of God through its own efforts or by means of any created thing, but only by divine light and by a special gift of divine grace. I believe there is no quicker or easier way for the soul to obtain this divine grace from God, supreme Good and supreme Love, than by a devout, pure, humble, continual, and violent prayer. . . . By prayer I mean not merely prayer from the mouth, but of the mind and heart, of all the powers of the soul and senses of the body. This is the prayer prayed by the soul who wills and desires to find this divine light, studying, meditating and reading without cease in the Book and the more-than-a-book of Life. This Book of Life is the entire life of Christ while he lived as a mortal on earth.

—Angela of Foligno

Hence we must say that for the knowledge of any truth whatsoever man needs divine help, that the intellect may be moved by God to its act. But he does not need a new light added to his natural light, in order to know the truth in all things, but only in some that surpasses his natural knowledge.

—Saint Thomas Aquinas

Be content to obey, which is never a small thing for the soul who has chosen God as his portion, and resign yourself to be for now a small hive bee able to make honey.

—Padre Pio

He who read much and understands much, receives his fill. He who is full, refreshes others. So Scripture says: "If the

clouds are full, they will pour rain upon the earth." Therefore, let your words be rivers, clean and limpid, so that you may charm the ears of people. And by the grace of your words win them over to follow your leadership. Solomon says: "The weapons of the understanding are the lips of the wise"; and in another place he says: "Let your lips be bound with wisdom." That is, let the meaning of your words shine forth, let understanding blaze out. Let no word escape your lips in vain or be uttered without depth of meaning.
—Saint Ambrose
from a letter

This intellect is so wild that it doesn't seem to be anything else than a frantic madman no one can tie down.
—Saint Theresa of Avila

All who undertake to teach must be endowed with deep love, the greatest of patience, and, most of all, profound humility. They must perform their work with earnest zeal. Then, through their humble prayers, the Lord will find them worthy to become fellow workers with him in the cause of truth. He will console them in the fulfillment of this most noble duty, and finally, will enrich them with the gift of heaven.

As Scripture says, "Those who instruct many in justice will shine as stars for all eternity." They will attain this more easily if they make a covenant of perpetual obedience and strive to cling to Christ and please him alone, because, in his words, "What you did to one of the least of my brethren, you did to me."
—Saint Joseph Calasanz

It does not follow that god is ignorant, since his knowledge is not of the genus of our knowledge; and therefore the op-

posite, ignorance, does not apply to him, just as one does not say of a stone that it has sight or is blind.
—Saint Thomas Aquinas

If ignorances are not purged within,
Hard effort will bring but small results.
You should thus strive to wipe out ignorance.
—Milarepa

If you do not know your mind,
What's the use of learning?
If in the void you cannot rest at ease,
Vain remarks will but increase your sins.
—Milarepa

The tree of life too may be understood as that more divine thought that has its origin in the world of sense, and the ascent through that to the originating and constructive cause of all. And this was the name He gave to every tree, implying fullness and indivisibility, and conveying only participation in what is good. But by the tree of the knowledge of good and evil, we are to understand that sensible and pleasurable food which, sweet though it seems, in reality brings him who partakes of it into communion with evil. For God says, "Of every tree in Paradise thou mayest freely eat." It is, me-thinks, as if God said, "Through all My creations thou art to ascend to Me thy creator, and the true life: let every thing bear for thee the fruit of life, and let participation in Me be the support of your own being. For in this way than wilt be immortal. But of the tree of the knowledge of good and evil, thou shall not eat of it: for in the day that thou eatest thereof thou shall surely die."
—Saint John of Damascus

EDUCATION

> The wise man does not unsettle
> the minds of the ignorant; quietly
> acting in the spirit of yoga,
> he inspires them to do the same.
> —Bhagavad Gita

As a youth, nay, almost as a boy not able to speak, I was taken captive, before I knew what to pursue and what to avoid. Hence to-day I blush and fear exceedingly to reveal my lack of education; for I am unable to tell my story to those versed in the art of concise writing—in such a way, I mean, as my spirit and mind long to do, and so that the sense of my words expresses what I feel.

But if indeed it had been given to me as it was given to others, then I would not be silent because of my desire of thanksgiving; and if perhaps some people think me arrogant for doing so in spite of my lack of knowledge and my slow tongue, it is, after all, written: The stammering tongues shall quickly learn to speak peace.
—Saint Patrick
from *The Confessions*

Section Twelve

MONEY

Like the physical body, money occupies much of our attention in this life. We need money in order to survive, we are afraid to lose it, we don't respect it, we waste it. It is no coincidence that spiritual students and saints of every practice are often encouraged to give up their worldly goods and donate what money they have to the needy. Those saints who detached from their money gained credibility with the faithful who understand the simplicity of life without it.

Scorn earthly trials with your whole soul; for all soldiers of Christ of either sex have despised temporal troubles and tempests and have held the frailties of this world as naught.
—Saint Boniface

Now observe the sun and the moon and stars and all the decoration of the greenness of the earth and consider how much prosperity God gives man with these things, although man sits with great temerity against God. . . . Who gives you a part in these bright and good things, if not God?
—Hildegard of Bingen

Lord, if I were rich I would willingly give a large sum of gold and silver, that by this means I might be absolved by these indulgences for the praise and glory of thy name.
—Saint Gertrude

Do not omit mental prayer for any occupation, for it is the sustenance of your soul.
—Saint John of the Cross

Remember always that everything that happens to you, whether prosperous or adverse, comes from God, so that you become neither puffed up in prosperity nor discouraged in adversity.
—Saint John of the Cross

Divine wisdom teaches this truth about poverty. It makes a person first see one's own defects, then discover one's own poverty and how truly one is poor in being. Thus illumined by the gift of divine grace, one sees the goodness of God.

Then all doubt concerning God is immediately taken away, and one loves God totally; and loving with this love one performs works in accordance with this love, and then all self-reliance is taken away....
—Angela of Foligno

The Sad Game

>Blame
>Keeps the sad game going.
>It keeps stealing all your wealth—
>Giving it to an imbecile with
>No financial skills.
>Dear one,
>Wise
>Up.
>
>—Hafiz

Even though the poor are often rough and unrefined, we must not judge them from external appearances nor from the mental gifts they seem to have received. On the contrary, if you consider the poor in the light of faith, then you will observe that they are taking the place of the Son of God who chose to be poor. Although in his passion he almost lost the appearance of a man and was considered a fool by the Gentiles and a stumbling block by the Jews, he showed them that his mission was to preach to the poor: "He sent me to preach the good news to the poor." We also ought to have this same spirit and imitate Christ's actions, that is, we must take care of the poor, console them, help them, support their cause.

Since Christ willed to be born poor, he chose for himself disciples who were poor. He made himself the servant of the poor and shared their poverty. He went so far as to say that he would consider every deed which either helps or

harms the poor as done for or against himself. Since God surely loves the poor, he also loves those who love the poor.
—Saint Vincent de Paul

With a new eye, a new ear, a new heart, whatever can be seen and heard is to be apprehended, by the faith and understanding of the disciples of the Lord, who speak, hear, and act spiritually. For there is genuine coin, and other that is spurious; which no less deceives unprofessionals, that it does not the money-changers; who know through having learned how to separate and distinguish what has a false stamp from what is genuine. So the money-changer only says to the unprofessional man that the coin is counterfeit. But the reason why, only the banker's apprentice, and he that is trained to this department, learns.
—Saint Clement of Alexandria

In prosperity, give thanks to God with humility and fear lest by pride you abuse God's benefits and so offend him.
—Saint Louis IX

If you seek an example of despising earthly things, follow him who is "the King of kings and the Lord of lords, in whom are hidden all the treasures of wisdom and knowledge." Upon the cross he was stripped, mocked, spat upon, struck, crowned with thorns, and given only vinegar and gall to drink.

Do not be attached, therefore, to clothing and riches, because "they divided my garments among themselves." Nor to honors, for he experienced harsh words and scourgings. Nor to greatness of rank, for "weaving a crown of thorns they placed it on my head." Nor to anything delightful, for "in my thirst they gave me vinegar to drink."
—Saint Thomas Aquinas

Souls are not given as gifts; they are bought. You do not know what they cost Jesus. Now they still have to be bought always with the same coin.
—Padre Pio

Jesus saw a man called Matthew sitting at the tax office, and he said to him: "Follow me." Jesus saw Matthew, not merely in the usual sense, but more significantly with his merciful understanding of men.

He saw the tax collector and, because he saw him through the eyes of mercy and chose him, he said to him: "Follow me." This following meant imitating the pattern of his life—not just walking after him. Saint John tells us: "Whoever says he abides in Christ ought to walk in the same way in which he walked."

And he rose and followed him. There is no reason for surprise that the tax collector abandoned earthly wealth as soon as the Lord commanded him. Nor should one be amazed that neglecting his wealth, he joined a band of men whose leader had, on Matthew's assessment, no riches at all. Our Lord summoned Matthew by speaking to him in words. By an invisible, interior impulse flooding his mind with the light of grace, he instructed him to walk in his footsteps. In this way Matthew could understand that Christ, who was summoning him away from earthly possessions, had incorruptible treasures of heaven in his gift.
—Saint Bede the Venerable
from a homily

The things which are seen are temporal; but the things which are not seen are eternal.
—Saint Luke

God has no need of your money, but the poor have. You give it to the poor, and God receives it.
—Saint Augustine of Hippo

The vow of poverty opens one's hands so that they let go of everything they were clutching. It fastens them securely so they can no longer reach toward the things of this world. It should also bind the hands of the spirit and the soul: the desires, which again and again reach for pleasures and things; the cares that want to secure earthly life in every respect; busyness about many things which endangers the one thing necessary.
—Edith Stein

All our religion is but a false religion, and all our virtues are mere illusions and we ourselves are only hypocrites in the sight of God, if we have not that universal charity for everyone—for the good, and for the bad, for the poor and for the rich, and for all those who do us harm as much as those who do us good.
—Saint John Mary Vianney

When the pearl is cast down in the mud it does not become dishonoured the more, nor if it is anointed with balsam oil will it become more precious. But it has its worth in the eyes of its owner at all times.
—Philip the Gnostic

> He who never thinks of
> Buddhahood, is angry,
> And anxious over money,
> Cannot a real Buddhist be.
> —Milarepa

If a man keeps dwelling on sense-objects,
attachment to them arises;
from attachment, desire flares up;
from desire, anger is born;

from anger, confusion follows;
from confusion, weakness of memory;
weak memory—weak understanding;
weak understanding—ruin.

But the man who is self-controlled,
who meets the objects of the senses
with neither craving nor aversion,
will attain serenity at last.
—Bhagavad Gita

Last night my teacher taught me the lesson of poverty, having nothing and wanting nothing.
—Rumi

For what is a man profited, if he shall gain the whole world, and lose his own soul? or what shall a man give in exchange for his soul?
—The Gospel
Saint Matthew 16:24–27

A person who desires perfection needs to undertake both internal and external action. In striving toward internal perfection, we must first practice the virtue of charity. When a person loves money, honors and good health, he does not always possess what he loves, whereas he who loves God possesses Him at once. Also, the soul needs patience. The virtue of patience maintains order in one's interior life. Love, joy and peace are virtues which perfect the soul with regard to what it possesses, while patience perfects it with regard to what it endures.
—Padre Pio

Section Thirteen

HOPE

The Catholic Encyclopedia defines *hope*, in its widest acceptation, as the desire of something together with the expectation of obtaining it. But hope is not so much a desire resulting from lack, but a desire arising from trust in God. Like faith and charity, it is thought to be directly and divinely implanted in the soul. We all have hope; it is a gift, a life preserver in the sea of spiritual despair. Saints of all religions understand the importance of hope in the life of a spiritual student: without hope, we have no access to divine grace.

Wherefore, people piling up for themselves worldly sadness, if they wish to overcome the wicked spirits urging them to it, and if they desire to flee this torment, if they live in the world should devote themselves to the spiritual life; or if they are already living as religious, let them fulfil the common discipline more than is usual, and submit themselves frequently to humble obedience, and ponder on the Scriptures which put before them celestial joy.
—Hildegard of Bingen

If you are indeed embracing patience in your mind and struggling to refuse tribulation, be assured, in fact you know, that there is no patience except in tribulation. Rejoice in tribulation, therefore, "knowing that tribulation causes patience, and patience approval, and approval hope, and hope does not confound."
—Saint Anselm of Canterbury

Rejoice and be glad always, for you shall not be put to shame.
—Saint Boniface

She had seen in her spiritual sight a palace of incredible greatness, in which were countless people, clad in white and shining clothes. And each of them seemed to have a proper seat to himself. In this palace stood principally a judgement seat, in which it was as if it were a sun; and the brightness that went from that sun was more than may otherwise be told or understood, in length, depth, and breadth. There stood also a virgin close to that seat, having a precious crown on her head. And all who were there served the

Son sitting on the throne, praising him with hymns and songs.
—Saint Birgitta

Hope, O my soul, hope. You know neither the day nor the hour. Watch carefully, for everything passes quickly, even though your impatience makes doubtful what is certain, and turns a very short time into a long one.
—Saint Teresa of Avila

We know certainly that our God calls us to a holy life. We know that he gives us every grace, every abundant grace; and though we are so weak of ourselves, this grace is able to carry us through every obstacle and difficulty.
—Elizabeth Ann Seton

It is God's will that we have three things in our seeking:
1. The first is that we seek earnestly and diligently, without sloth, and, as it may be through His grace, without unreasonable heaviness and vain sorrow.
2. The second is, that we abide Him steadfastly for His love, without murmuring and striving against Him, to our life's end: for it shall last but awhile.
3. The third is that we trust in Him mightily of full-assured faith. For it is His will that we know that He shall appear suddenly and blissfully to all that love Him.
—Julian of Norwich

An Invisible Pile of Wood

It
Is often
Nothing the Master says

That keeps the desired fire in me
Alive

Wherever the Master goes
An invisible pile of wood tags along

That he keeps throwing logs from
Onto my

Soul's hearth

—Hafiz

Every moment the sunlight is totally empty and totally full.
—Rumi

Act of Hope
   For your mercies' sake, O Lord my God, tell me what you are to me. Say to my soul: "I am your salvation." So speak that I may hear, O Lord; my heart is listening; open it that it may hear you, and say to my soul: "I am your salvation." After hearing this word, may I come in haste to take hold of you. Hide not your face from me. Let me see your face even if I die, lest I die with longing to see it. The house of my soul is too small to receive you; let it be enlarged by you. It is all in ruins; do you repair it. There are things in it—I confess and I know—that must offend your sight. But who shall cleanse it? Or to what others besides you shall I cry out? From my secret sins cleanse me, O Lord, and from those of others spare your servant.
Amen.

—Saint Augustine of Hippo

A priest was once preaching on hope, and on the mercy of the good God. He reassured others, but he himself despaired. After the sermon, a young man presented himself, saying, "Father, I am come to confess to you:" The priest answered, "I am willing to hear your confession:" The other recounted his sins, after which he added, "Father, I have done much evil; I am lost!" "What do you say, my friend! We must never despair:" The young man rose, saying, "Father, you wish me not to despair, and what do you do?" This was a ray of light; the priest, all astonishment, drove away that thought of despair, became a religious and a great saint.... The good God had sent him an angel under the form of a young man, to show him that we must never despair. The good God is as prompt to grant us pardon when we ask it of Him as a mother is to snatch her child out of the fire.

—Saint John Vianney

Do not ever lose heart when the tempest rages; place all your trust in the Heart of the most gentle Jesus. Pray and I might add, devoutly pester the divine Heart.

—Padre Pio

We ought to understand that while God knows all things beforehand, yet He does not predetermine all things. For He knows beforehand those things that are in our power, but He does not predetermine them. For it is not His will that there should be wickedness nor does He choose to compel virtue. So that predetermination is the work of the divine command based on fore-knowledge. But on the other hand God predetermines those things which are not within our power in accordance with His prescience. For already God in His prescience has prejudged all things in accordance with His goodness and justice.

—Saint John of Damascus

O Lord and Vivifier, your grace has achieved for us all that you had spoken and promised.

Grant us access to the place of your peace. For you are our Vivifier, you are our Consoler, you are our life Remedy, you are our Standard of Victory.

Blessed are we, O Lord, because we have known you!

Blessed are we, because we have believed in you!

Blessed are we, because we bear your wounds and the sign of your blood on our countenances!

Blessed are we, because you are our great hope!

Blessed are we, because you are our God forever!
—Acts of Thomas

The first thing one has to do is to keep his mind calm. An eye that never stops roaming about, looking sideways and up and down without stopping, will never see anything very clearly; if it wants to have a good look at any visible object it has to let its glance rest on it for a while. In the same way a man's mind that is distracted by all the concerns of the world cannot find the way to concentrate on the truth.... There is only one way to get away from these evils, and that is to separate oneself entirely from the world. But to withdraw from the world does not mean to leave it bodily; it means to break the bonds that tie the soul to the body. Then one can be without city or house or goods of one's own, without particular friendships, without possessions or livelihood, no business, no contracts, no study of human learning; but ready to take to heart the divine teaching imprinted within oneself.
—Saint Basil the Great
from a letter to Gregory of Nazianzus

God immediately affects all things so that nothing other [than God] is the cause of anything. This is so

much the case that they claim that fire does not burn but God [is the cause]; nor is the hand moved except as God causes its motion, and so with other examples. This position, however, is stupid since it removes order from the universe and takes away from things their proper activity and does away with the judgement of [our] senses.
—Saint Thomas Aquinas

Different people call on [God] by different names: some as Allah, some as God, and others as Krishna, Siva, and Brahman. It is like the water in a lake. Some drink it at one place and call it "jal," others at another place and call it "pani," and still others at a third place and call it "water." The Hindus call it "jal," the Christians "water," and the Moslems "pani." But it is one and the same thing.
—Sri Ramakrishna

And even the very continuity of the creation, and its preservation and governance, teach us that there does exist a Deity, who supports and maintains and preserves and ever provides for this universe. For how could opposite natures, such as fire and water, air and earth, have combined with each other so as to form one complete world, and continue to abide in indissoluble union, were there not some omnipotent power which bound them together and always is preserving them from dissolution?
—Saint John of Damascus

> When you realize it you will never
> fall back into delusion;
> knowing it, you see all beings
> in yourself, and yourself in me.

Even if you were the most evil
of evildoers, Arjuna,
wisdom is the boat that would carry you
across the sea of all sin.

Just as firewood is turned
to ashes in the flames of a fire,
all actions are turned to ashes
in wisdom's refining flames.

—Bhagavad Gita

Do not disturb your soul at the sad spectacle of human injustice.... One day you will see the inevitable triumph of Divine justice over it.

—Padre Pio

God sends helpers too when he sees fit, and all we can do is just keep praying for them.

—Dorothy Day

No one can be saved without divine light. Divine light causes us to begin and to make progress, and it leads us to the summit of perfection. Therefore if you want to begin and to receive this divine light, pray. If you have begun to make progress and want this light to be intensified within you, pray. And if you have reached the summit of perfection, and want to be super-illumined so as to remain in that state, pray.

—Angela of Foligno

BIOGRAPHICAL NOTES ON THE SOURCES

Saint Alphais

(?–1211)

Alphais was born poor and spent her childhood in bed with leprosy, which possibly gave rise to her penitent nature and her commitment to holy work. While not much is known about her, she had enough of a public cult following to be named a saint.

Blessed Alphonsa of India

(1910–1946)

Alphonsa was generally sickly throughout her life and died young from stomach troubles. Known for her quiet nature, she taught grammar school and endeared herself to the children with her gentleness. Almost immediately upon her death, Alphonsa began appearing to children in visions. She is known as the patron saint of the sick.

Saint Alphonsus de Liguori

(1696–1787)

Alphonsus was a lawyer before he became a priest, bishop, and a then saint whose down-to-earth style and firm doctrine revealed themselves in his writings. He published *Moral Theology* in order to show Christians a middle route between rigor and laziness.

Saint Ambrose, Bishop of Milan

(340–397)
Ambrose won the vote for Bishop much to his own surprise, but soon rose to the occasion by divesting himself of his wealth and parlaying his previous love for the law into administrating and preaching Christianity. Loved and esteemed by many, Ambrose's powerful and compelling version of the teachings of Christ converted Saint Augustine of Hippo.

Angela of Foligno

(1248–1309)
Angela married a wealthy man and reveled in material possessions and a pleasure-seeking life before experiencing an about-face and committing to a life of poverty. At age thirty-seven, Angela modeled herself after Saint Francis of Assisi, divesting herself of her possessions, making a pilgrimage to Assisi, and hoping to meet Christ in the poor. Her writings include *The Book of Divine Consolations of the Blessed Angela of Foligno* and *The Book of Visions and Instructions*, both of which drew from her spiritual visions.

Father Annibale di Francia

(1851–1927)
Born in Sicily, a son of the Italian nobility, he was ordained a priest in 1878. In 1910, he traveled to Corato, Italy, where he began a seventeen-year series of visits and an intensely spiritual relationship with a young woman named Luisa, who frequently saw visions of Jesus and Mary. He founded the Rogationist Fathers of the Heart of Jesus and the Daughters of Divine Zeal, and in 1926 he was designated ecclesiastical censor for the united dioceses of Trani, Varletta, and Bisceglie.

Saint Anselm of Canterbury

(1033–1109)
Anselm grew up in an era of political and spiritual unrest; in the tenth century, the papacy was weak and emperors dominated. He was an outstanding philosopher and theologian, as well as a gentle and humble teacher in the monastery where he lived for forty-nine years. As the Archbishop of Canterbury, he inspired his monks and the society around them. Anselm is thought of as the more important Christian thinker between Saint Augustine and Saint Thomas Aquinas.

Augustine of Hippo

(354–430)
Augustine became a renowned writer and teacher of Christian thought throughout Rome and North Africa, but not before battling his era's philosphical and academic skepticism towards the metaphysical. Struggling for three years, he eventually read the Holy Scriptures and listened to Saint Ambrose, both of which convinced him that Jesus Christ is the only way to truth and salvation. His *Confessions* describes his interior journey to God.

Saint Augustine of Canterbury

Roman monk (?–ca. 606)
He brought Christianity to England in the sixth century and became the first archbishop of Canterbury. Augustine had lived a monastic life of work, prayer, and study of Scriptures. In response to Pope Gregory's directive to take the gospel message to the Anglo-Saxons, Augustine went to England and won the king's permission to convert all who would listen. His evangelization in southeastern England would grow throughout the entire British Isles.

Saint Basil the Great

(329–379)
Basil was respected and loved for his aggressive attitude. At twenty-two he went to Athens for five years to further his liberal education, and there he met Gregory of Nazianzus, a fellow student, with whom he formed a lifelong friendship. He returned to his home state of Pontus and started a monastic community around his family's estate. Basil is known as "the great" because he successfully defended the freedom of the church from the greedy power of the state.

Saint Bede the Venerable

(673–735)
Bede was raised in the Wearmouth Abbey and lived there his whole life. He was deeply committed to the church, believing it had the power to convert cultural violence, and took pleasure in writing, teaching, and study. He served as a priest, a Benedictine monk, teacher, and writer, translating the gospel of John and writing a history of the church, *Historia Ecclesiastica*. His writings started the idea of dating this era from the incarnation of Christ.

Bhagavad Gita

Ancient Hindu spiritual text written by an unknown saint of India between the fifth century B.C. and the first century A.D. The Bhagavad Gita, a single chapter of a larger work, the Mahabharata, is considered by Eastern and Western scholars alike to be among the world's greatest spiritual books. In essence, it is a conversation between Lord Krishna and Arjuna framed in a battle story. Lord Krishna describes the science of self-realization and the exact process by which a human being can establish an eternal relationship with God.

Saint Bernard of Clairvaux

(1090–1153)
Saint Bernard joined the abbey of Citeaux at age twenty-two, along with his brothers and several friends looking for sanctuary from the world. He founded and led a Benedictine monastery at Clairvaux which became home to hundreds of monks. His religious work lay in politics, advising as well as admonishing the kings of France, helping to organize the second crusade, and helping to end the schism of anti–Pope Anacletus II.

Saint Birgitta

(ca. 1302–1373)
Birgitta began receiving visions, mostly of the Crucifixion, at age seven. Her mother, known for her piety, died c. 1315 when the girl was about twelve years old, and she was raised and educated by an equally pious aunt. She was arranged to marry a prince at age thirteen, becoming a princess and the mother of eight children, including Saint Catherine of Sweden. While married and a mother, she pursued her religious calling by becoming friend and counselor to many priests and theologians. When her husband died she returned to a more devout religious life, renouncing her title and recording the revelations given her in her visions, and these became hugely popular in the Middle Ages.

Saint Bonaventure

(1221–1274)
In his early twenties Bonaventure moved to Paris where he joined the Franciscan Order of Friars Minor and taught Franciscan theology. His early writings came from this period and established him as a leading authority on Fran-

ciscan thought, as well as changed the contemporary opinion that medieval theologians were dry rationalists. Many of Bonaventure's writings delved deeply into spirituality.

Saint Boniface

(c. 673–754)
Boniface was educated at the Benedictine monastery at Exeter in England. He was a missionary to Germany in 719, where there were only scattered centers of Christian influence. There is a story that when in Saxony, Boniface encountered a tribe worshipping a Norse deity in the form of a huge oak, reportedly six feet across. Boniface removed his shirt, picked up an axe, and without a word hacked down the tree. Never afraid to discuss his disappointment with church authorities, he died a martyr's death in Holland.

Saint Brigid

(453–523)
A legendary saint about whom more myth exists than fact, Brigid was a beloved character in Ireland for generosity which drove her to give away valuables to anyone who asked. She was the daughter of a slavewoman and a chieftain and heard the call to become a nun but used her instincts to gather other women together in religious communities. She started convents all over Ireland and invented the double monastery, a retreat for both monks and nuns.

Saint Camillus de Lellis

(1550–1614)
Before becoming a priest, Camillus was a renowned rebel and fought in the Venetian army. He was persuaded by a Capuchin Friar to convert to Christ only after he literally

lost everything he owned to gambling. He worked in and reformed hospitals for the incurably sick in Rome and founded the Congregation of the Servants of the Sick (the Camellians).

Saint Catherine of Siena

(1347–1380)
The Italian mystic was a peacemaker, active in political affairs and counselor to the pope as she influenced him to return from Avignon to Rome. By the time she was 20, Catherine had become so widely known for her personal holiness and asceticism—she regularly begged for money and baked bread for the poor and hungry— that she attracted a group of spiritual disciples—priests and laymen, men and women.

Saint Clement of Alexandria

(ca. 150–215)
Saint Clement was an early Greek theologian and began his career as a "pagan" philosopher as the head of the catechetical school of Alexandria. After converting to Christianity he traveled extensively throughout Europe to study with highly respected Christian teachers. He is author of the largest body of Christian works in the second century. In the *Miscellanies* Clement leads Christians to a higher understanding of the mysteries of God.

Dorothy Day

(1897–1980)
Dorothy Day's life was itself a radical movement. In the 1930s, she and Peter Maurin cofounded the Catholic Worker Movement. As a journalist, Day lived through and commented on the central events of the twentieth century: wars,

economic depression, class struggle, the nuclear threat, and the civil rights movement. *The Catholic Worker* and her prodigious writings have always focused the light of the Gospel on our struggles of conscience. She is in the process of being canonized by the Catholic Church.

Saint Elizabeth of the Trinity

(1880–1906)
A lively, deeply religious, and stubborn woman, Elizabeth took Christ as her spouse at the age of fourteen, making a private vow of virginity and entering the convent at twenty-one. Noted for great spiritual growth, Elizabeth frequently wrote of her delight in immersing herself in God, explaining in a letter to a friend that taking the name "Elizabeth of the Trinity" allowed herself to be cloistered, to disappear into God, to be invaded by the three (of the Trinity).

Saint Francis of Assisi

(1181–1226)
Francis was more of a warrior than a benevolent romantic, though he was ultimately known for his kindness, holiness, and founding of the Franciscan order. Before giving up all of his wealth and worldly belongings to serve Christ, Francis fought as a knight, thinking battle to be a way of serving a larger force. When he was about twenty, Francis answered a voice he heard saying: "Go, Francis, and repair my house, which as you see is falling into ruin." This began a long process of repairing the church as an institution.

Saint Francis de Sales

(1567–1622)
Francis was a priest and preacher who converted Protestants by traveling and evangelizing, becoming an impor-

tant leader in the Catholic Reformation. In *Introduction to the Devout Life*, Francis wrote about how ordinary people locked into the worldly, mundane life might live a holy and even saintly life. Living for God, he believed, brought meaning to every vocation.

Saint Gertrude

(1256–1302)
As a young girl, Gertrude had a gentle disposition and a voracious appetite for learning. She was fluent in Latin at an early age and regularly read (and believed in) philosophy, that is, until she had a vision in which Christ reproached her for becoming too enamored with secular thinking. Her sisters in the Abbey knew she was favored by God, and often appealed to her for help with their sins. Some said that simply being around and praying to Gertrude redeemed them.

Saint Gregory the Great

(540–604)
In just thirteen short years as pope, Gregory accomplished a litany of important political and religious feats. He rebuilt a barbarian-ravaged Rome, rescued it from famine and plague, resisted and withstood the Byzantine empire, promoted the Benedictine monastic life, and initiated the conversion of England to Christianity. He also wrote and collected hymns which we now know as Gregorian chants.

Hafiz

(1320–1389)
A beloved Sufi mystic and poet who lived and wrote during the same era as English poet Geoffrey Chaucer. Hafiz means "memorizer," a name given to an individual who memorized the entire Quran.

Hildegard of Bingen

(1098–1179)
Hildegard, the tenth child of a noble family, suffered precarious health as a child and had her first vision before the age of five. Her family chose the ascetic route and committed Hildegard for "life" to the cell of an anchoress named Jutta, the pious daughter of a count who had devoted her life to spiritual teachings. There she studied with a number of women in what became a Benedictine convent. After Jutta died, Hildegard became the head of the convent. Commanded in a blinding epiphany to "say and write what you hear," Hildegard published many works that made her famous through Germany and beyond.

Saint Jeanne Frances de Chantal

(1572–1641)
Though she served God her entire life, Jeanne forever battled nagging doubt in her soul. (Today she might have been diagnosed as clinically depressed.) After her husband died she met Francis de Sales, who convinced her to build with him a religious community just for women. She founded the Order of the Visitation of Our Lady for widows and laywomen who did not wish the full life of the orders, and she oversaw the founding of sixty-nine convents.

Saint Jerome

(347–419)
Though highly educated in Greek and Roman literature, Jerome led a misspent youth. He studied to become a lawyer before he began his study of theology, living for years as a monk and a hermit in the Syrian deserts. He was known for his bitter disposition, but his translation of the Old and New Testaments were used in Western churches for centuries.

Saint Joan of Arc

(1412-1431)
At the age of thirteen and a half, in the summer of 1425, Joan first became conscious of what she came to call her "voices" or her "counsel," which asked that she go to the aid of the king of France. Surprising her war-torn nation with her bravery, she successfully led an army to force the English out of France, though she was later persecuted as a heretic by the French government. During her trial for heresy she only wore men's clothing, so as to remind the government she was being tried as a warrior, not as a woman. Her clothing deeply disturbed the clergy and government officials and she was martyred, though later she was canonized.

Saint John the Apostle

(?–101)
St. John the Apostle and Evangelist, commonly known as John the Baptist, was called the "beloved disciple" perhaps because Jesus wanted him around during significant moments, proving his trust in John. John was the only one of the Twelve Apostles who followed Jesus to the cross and remained there at the hour of this death. Jesus asked him to care for his mother, Mary. He is thought to have written the fourth Gospel, three Epistles, and the Book of Revelation.

Saint John Bosco

(1815-1888)
John had a penchant for the extraordinary. Guided by dreams and skilled in people's minds, John was an evangelist, educator, and leader of great faith. In 1841 as a newly ordained priest he came to Turin, Italy, and encouraged

abandoned children to participate in fun, games, food, catechism, and worship.

Saint John of the Cross

(1542–1591)
John was born in poverty and became a Carmelite brother by age twenty-one and a Carmelite priest at age twenty-five. He was persuaded by Saint Theresa of Avila to begin the "barefoot reform" within the Carmelite order, which was not well received by some of the brotherhood. As a consequence John was imprisoned, but he escaped after less than a year to continue work on the contemplative spiritual writings he had earlier begun. In 1926, Pope Pius XI named John a doctor of the church.

Saint John of Damascus

(676–787)
Raised in Greece, John of Damascus was an intellectual of similar caliber to Thomas of Aquinas. He was tutored in his youth by an Italian monk and attended Muslim schools, becoming vastly educated in both Christian thought and the classical fields of geometry, literature, logic, and rhetoric. His writings are held in the highest esteem in both the Catholic and Greek churches. He is the author of *The Fountain of Wisdom*, the first real summary of Christian theology and the teachings of the Greek fathers.

Saint John of God

(1495–1550)
John was a shepherd who spent a wild youth traveling Europe as a soldier and mercenary before he went to Africa as a missionary. Returning to Spain to open a religious book-

shop where he hoped to lead others to Christ, he suffered a brief period in a mental hospital before he began caring for the sick, poor, and homeless. He founded the Order of Charity and the Order of Hospitallers.

Saint John Mary Vianney

(1786–1859)
John was not formerly educated but possessed extraordinary moral intelligence and deep, intuitive understanding of Christianity. He became a priest at age thirty and was assigned to a tiny parish with poor attendance in rural France where he eventually drew thousands and spent forty years. People responded with zeal to his blend of strictness and gentleness.

Saint Joseph Cafasso

(1811–1860)
Joseph lived with a disabling spine injury but nevertheless came to be loved as a popular lecturer. He worked to reform prisoners and to improve prison conditions in and around Turin, Italy. He ministered to violent prisoners who lived in barbarous conditions. He taught his students to speak colloquially in order to better communicate with their subjects, much as Christ had done.

Saint Joseph Calasanz

(1556–1648)
Joseph was the youngest of five children. After one of his brother's and his mother's death, Joseph's future took a turn toward God. Though his father wanted him to become a soldier, to marry, and to continue the family, the death of his loved ones and his own near fatal illness caused Joseph to seriously examine his life, and he defied

his father's wishes and devoted himself fervently to the religious life.

Julian of Norwich

(1342–1413)
Not much is known about this English mystic, but that she lived as a recluse. Believing God had given her a revelation to all Christians, she hid herself away so as not to draw attention to herself, to write, and urge readers to focus on God only. Her book, *Revelations of Divine Love*, contains sixteen revelations that she received while in ecstatic trance. These visions conveyed to her that God was love, and living a life devoted to God meant living his love as law.

Saint Julie Billiart

(1751–1816)
At age fourteen she took a private vow of chastity and gave her life to serving and teaching the poor. She was a natural teacher; even when her family slid into poverty she still found time to instruct others in faith while working. At age twenty-two, she was sitting next to her father when someone shot at him; the shot missed, but the trauma of the event caused her to contract a mysterious illness that left her paralyzed for twenty-two years. Even so, she helped found the Institute of Notre Dame, a community of women devoted to caring for and instructing poor girls.

Saint Louis IX

(1214–1270)
In unusual behavior for a King, Louis put God first, praying hours a day and only waging war in order to facilitate peace. King of France for forty-four years, he presided over France's spiritual and cultural renaissance during the Middle

Ages. He became known for his just judgment, his founding of monasteries and building of leper hospitals. He led two crusades against Muslim invaders, dying of typhoid on the second one.

Saint Luke

(first century)
Born Greek, Luke worked as a doctor before converting to the teachings of Jesus, largely owing to the Apostle Paul's evangelism. He embarked on evangelical travels with Paul to Greece and Rome and is believed to have written the Gospel According to Luke, much of which focussed on themes of prayer and compassion. Luke also wrote a history of the early Church in the Acts of the Apostles in an excellent popular prose style and, it is said, with fastidious fact-checking sensibility. He died a martyr in Greece.

Maimonides

(1135–1204)
Jewish commentator and philosopher in Egypt who devoted himself to the exposition of the Talmud. The principle that inspired all his philosophical activity was that there can be no contradiction between the truths that God revealed and the findings of the human mind in science and philosophy.

Blessed Maria Gabriella

(1914–1939)
Maria was an obstinate child whose disposition changed when she turned eighteen. She became gentle, more thoughtful, and inward-looking. A sensitivity concerning the Church and the needs of the apostolate caused her to enroll in "Catholic Action," a Church-sponsored youth movement.

At twenty-one she entered the Trappestine monastery, offering her life to God.

Blessed Marie-Rose Durocher

(1811–1849)
Marie-Rose was the tenth of eleven children in a Canadian family. At the age of nineteen, she went to live with her brother, Reverend Theophile Durocher, in his rectory. Here her love for prayer, sense of charity, and concern for the lack of Christian education among young people helped make her name. Marie-Rose helped found the Sisters of the Holy Names of Jesus and Mary with her two companions, Henriette Cere and Melodie Dufresne.

Saint Mary Magdalen de' Pazzi

(1566–1607)
Strikingly beautiful and born to Florence's nobility, Mary made her own First Communion at the age of ten, and shortly afterward vowed her virginity to God. She had an extreme disposition despite her life of service in a convent, suffering from a mysterious illness, battling lust and gluttony, at times losing herself in prayer for months, and at other times contemplating suicide because she believed God had abandoned her.

Saint Matthew

(second century)
Matthew was a Jew who worked for Rome as a tax collector before serving Christ as an Apostle. Matthew is thought to have preached among the Jews for fifteen years, possibly in enclaves in Ethiopia and even farther east. The authorship and time of composition of the Gospel of Saint Matthew are open to question, but whoever the actual author, Matthew's

Gospel is the first in the canon of the New Testament, and it was written in part to convince Jewish readers that their anticipated Messiah had come in the person of Jesus.

Saint Maximilian Kolbe

(1894–1941)
Maximilian called himself a "knight" of Mary, seeing himself as fighting at her side against the darkness engulfing the world. An outspoken opponent of the Nazis, Maximilian was imprisoned in Auschwitz for his anti-Nazi publications. He died when he traded places with a young married man who was to be slaughtered in retribution for aiding an escaped prisoner. In the 1960s, his insights into Marian theology influenced Vatican II.

Milarepa

(ca. 1050–1145)
Milarepa was a yogi, sage, and poet much-beloved by the Tibetan people. He taught Buddhist wisdom through his songs and was said to be an exemplar of an ordinary person who attains enlightenment in a single lifetime.

Mira Bai

(1498–1547)
An Indian Brahman woman who left riches to walk barefoot lost in love of Krishna. Mira Bai belonged to the strong tradition of bhakti (devotional) poets in medieval India, who expressed their love of God through the love for a child, for a friend, or for a beloved.

Naropa and Tilopa

(tenth century)
Naropa was a scholar in India who went on a long pilgrim-

age in search of the great master Tilopa, from whom he eventually learned extensive Buddhist teachings. In the Eastern religious tradition of spiritual teacher bringing the student into spiritual knowledge, Tilopa taught Naropa by shocking his mind to eliminate the mental conditions that kept him in a state of suffering, a result, according to Buddhism, of ordinary humanity. During his education, Naropa offered a mandala (sacred image) to Tilopa, requesting him to give empowerment. From then on, whenever Naropa offered a mandala to his teacher, Tilopa showed him a sign.

Saint Patrick

(387– 493)
At age sixteen, Patrick was carried off into captivity by Irish marauders and was sold as a slave to a chieftain, meant to tend his pigs. During his six years in captivity, he acquired a perfect knowledge of the Celtic tongue and also prayed his way into Christian maturity. Even after he escaped captivity, Patrick knew he was destined to return to the land with which he had fallen in love. He went back as a bishop, winning protection of the pagan priests and then converting thousands.

Saint Paul

(3–65)
Born a Jew, Paul despised and persecuted Christians as heretical and even assisted at the stoning of Saint Stephen before having the mystical experience that converted him to Christianity. On his way to Damascus to arrest a group of heretics, he was knocked to the ground, struck blind, and given the message that in persecuting Christians, he was persecuting Christ. He converted instantly, was baptized,

and began traveling and preaching throughout the eastern Mediterranean countryside. He was beheaded in the year 65 during the persecutions of Nero.

Saint Peter Claver

(1581–1654)

A farmer's son who became a Jesuit priest, he worked as a missionary in the Americas, ministering physically and spiritually to slaves, overcoming his revulsion of their tortured conditions by kissing and licking their open sores. He was thought to have baptized hundreds of thousands of slaves in forty years.

Philip the Gnostic

(second century)

From A.D. 68, Philip was part of an Essene community that comprised some of the earliest followers of Christ. He is considered a Gnostic, aware of the New Testament text, but not participating in the theology of the New Testament.

Padre Pio

(1887–1968)

Padre Pio was born Francesco Forgione in Pietrelcina, a small town in southern Italy. He was a shepherd until he heard the calling of the priesthood and was sent by his father to America to study. At the age of fifteen he entered the novitiate of the Capuchin Friars. In 1918, the five wounds of Jesus' Passion reportedly appeared on his body, making him the first stigmatized priest in the known history of the Catholic Church. Over the course of his career, he organized and led significant programs meant to relieve the suffering of the sick and the poor. His works were largely carried out with the help of disciples and the small spontaneous financial offerings of his massive following of devotees and believers from all over the world. His canonization is imminent.

Sri Ramakrishna

(1836–1886)
A beloved Indian sage who proclaimed the oneness of all religions and the worship of the blissful Divine Mother. His life was an uninterrupted contemplation of God, and he embodies the core of the spiritual realizations of the seers and sages of India. As he faithfully practiced the spiritual disciplines of different religions, Ramakrishna came to the realization that all of them led to the same goal, an endorsement of religious freedom. Thus he declared, "As many faiths, so many paths."

Saint Rose of Lima

(1617–1671)
Born as Isabel in the New World, Rose modeled her piety after that of Saint Catherine of Siena, fasting often and praying for several hours a day. She was so devoted to her vow of chastity that she used pepper to ruin her complexion so she would not be attractive. She lived and meditated in a garden, raising vegetables and making embroidered items to sell to support her family. She made an infirmary in her home to help the poor.

Rumi

(1207–1273)
A Sufi mystic whose influence on thought, literature, and all forms of aesthetic expression in the world of Islam cannot be overstated. He was introduced to the mystical path

by a wandering dervish, Shamsuddin of Tabriz. His love and his bereavement for the death of Shamsuddin found expression in a surge of music, dance, and beautiful, lyrical poems. Underlying all of Rumi's work is the absolute love of God.

Elizabeth Ann Seton

(1774–1821)
Elizabeth was the first American woman to be beatified; she had left her Protestant heritage to become Catholic. After her beloved husband's death, she opened a school for girls in Maryland which gathered a strong community of women, and she eventually formed the Sisters of Charity. The sisters initiated the parochial school system and established orphanages up and down the East coast.

Edith Stein

(1891–1942)
Hidden in a convent during a time when the world around her was caught up in Hitler's fiery persecution of Jews, Edith Stein's writings reveal both her awareness of the fire and her vision of the cross rising above it. She became a member of the Carmelite community in Echt, Holland. Her faith and surrender has led the Church to declare this woman blessed.

Saint Teresa of Avila

(1515–?)
Teresa did not become serious about her spiritual life until her forties, when a series of visitations from Christ launched her spiritual growth. She suffered the same problem that Francis of Assisi did—she was too charming. Her books on

prayer were considered both practical and profound, and in part because of those qualities she earned the title Doctor of the Church in 1622.

Mother Teresa of Calcutta

(1910–1997)
Born Agnes Gonxha Bojaxhiu in Skopje in Macedonia, she went to India at age eighteen, where she came across a half-dead woman lying in front of a Calcutta hospital. Teresa stayed at her side until she died. From then on, she dedicated her life to helping the poorest of the poor in India, thus gaining her the name "Saint of the Gutters." She founded an order of nuns called the Missionaries of Charity in Calcutta, India. The Missionaries of Charity have grown from twelve sisters in India to over three thousand in 517 missions throughout one hundred countries worldwide. She is the saint who has achieved the most global popularity, and she won the Nobel Peace Prize in 1979.

Terese of the Andes

(1900–1920)
From her adolescence, Terese was a mystic who was devoted to Christ. After entering a nunnery in 1919, she became a model of devotion for young people and was honored with the name Teresa of Jesus. She was the first Chilean and the first member of the Teresian Carmelites in Latin America to be beatified.

Saint Thérèse of Lisieux

(1873–1897)
At age fifteen, Thérèse Martin entered the convent of Lisieux. The account of the eleven years of her religious life, marked by signal graces and constant growth in holiness, is

written in her autobiography, *A Story of a Soul,* which attracted millions with its simplicity. She died at twenty-four from tuberculosis, before realizing her dream of becoming a missionary.

Saint Thomas Aquinas

(1225–1274)

Philosopher, theologian, patron of Catholic universities, colleges, and schools, Thomas was diligent in study and was thus early noted as being meditative and devoted to prayer. His preceptor was surprised at hearing the child frequently ask: "What is God?"

On December 6, 1273, he experienced a divine revelation that so enraptured him that he abandoned the Summa, saying it and his other writing were so much straw in the wind compared to the reality of the divine glory. He died four months later, overweight and with his health broken by overwork.

His works have been seminal to the thinking of the Church ever since as they systematized her great thoughts and teaching, and combined Greek wisdom and scholarship methods with the truth of Christianity.

Saint Thomas More

(1478–1535)

Thomas was a layperson; a married man, a happy head of the household, a writer, and a friend of King Henry VIII. He was Lord Chancellor of England—a position of power second only to the king. He opposed the king on the matter of royal divorce, and refused to swear the Oath of Supremacy which declared the king the head of the Church in England. Thomas was imprisoned, then beheaded for his refusal to bend his religious beliefs to the king's political needs.

Thomas the Apostle

(?– ca. 72)
Saint Thomas is remembered for his exhibit of conflicting faith and doubt. When he learned of Christ's Resurrection from the other Apostles, he did not believe it possible— until eight days later he put his own hands in Christ's wounds. Some say he later carried the gospel to India.

Saint Vincent de Paul

(1580–1660)
As a priest, Vincent spent his early years ministering in the prosperous countryside outside of Paris. He learned from a wealthy family, for whom he tutored, that his spiritual mission would be evangelizing to the rich and entreating them to serve the poor.

Swami Vivekananda

(1863–1902)
A disciple of one of India's most renowned holy men, Ramakrishna, he claimed that all religions are true. He aimed to integrate the world's highest religious teachings with a universal approach to Vedanta, the prevalent religion in India from 1500 B.C. to 500 B.C. Swami Vivekananda is responsible for bringing the yoga philosophy to the West at the World's Parliament of Religions, held in Chicago in 1893.

BIBLIOGRAPHY

Angela of Foligno. *Angela of Foligno: Complete Works.* New Jersey: Paulist Press, 1993.
Augustine of Hippo. *The Confessions of Saint Augustine.* New York: Doubleday & Co., 1972.
Barks, Coleman, trans. *The Essential Rumi.* New York: HarperCollins, 1995.
Benedicta, Sister Teresa of the Cross Discalced Carmelite. L. Gelber and Michael Linssen, eds. *Collected Works of Bl. Edith Stein—The Hidden Life: Hagiographic Essays, Meditations, Spiritual Texts.* Washington, D.C.: ICS Publications, 1992.
Bowler, Joseph D., ed. *Saint Francis of Sales: Introduction to the Devout Life—A Popular Abridgment.* Chicago: Tan Books, 1992.
Saint Bonaventure (Giovanni di Fidanza). *The Journey of the Mind into God*, Quarrachi Edition of the *Opera Omnia S. Bonaventurae.* Grand Rapids, Mich.: Christian Classics Ethereal Library, 2000. www.ccel.org/b/bonaventure/journey/journey.html
Catholic Community Forum. www.catholic~forum.com
Chang, Garma C. C., trans. *The Hundred Thousand Songs of Milarepa.* Boulder and London: Shambhala Publications, 1977.
Clark, Mary T., ed. *An Aquinas Reader.* New York: Fordham University Press, 2000.
Clement of Alexandria. *The Stromata, or Miscellanies.* Electronic version copyright New Advent, Inc., 1996. www.newadvent.org/fathers/0210.htm

Day, Dorothy. "On Pilgrimage—March 1966." *The Catholic Worker*. New York, 1966. www.catholicworker.org/dorothy day/
De' Liguori, Alfonso Maria. *The Glories of Mary*. St. Louis: Liguori Publications, 2000.
de Voragine, Jacobus, ed., William Granger Ryan, trans. *The Golden Legend: Readings on the Saints*, vols. I and II. Princeton, N.J.: Princeton University Press, 1995.
Francis of Assisi: The Little Flowers of St. Francis of Assisi, Raphael Brown, trans. Garden City, N.Y.: Image Books, 1958.
Geisler, Norman L., ed. *What Augustine Says*. Grand Rapids, Mich: Baker Book House, 1982.
Guenther, Herbert V., trans. *The Life and Teaching of Naropa*. Oxford: Clarendon Press, 1963.
Hixon, Lex, trans. *The Great Swan: Meetings with Ramakrishna*. Boston: Shambhala Publications, 1992.
Howlett, D. R., ed. *The Confessions of Saint Patrick*. St. Louis: Liguori Publications, 1996.
Ilford, Mary and Walter Nigg, eds. *Warriors of God: the Great Religious Orders and Their Founders*. New York: Alfred A. Knopf, 1959.
Julian of Norwich, Grace Warrack, ed. *Revelations of Divine Love*, London: Methuen & Co., 1901. www.ccel.wheaton.edu/julian/revelations/
Kavanaugh, Kieran and Otilio Rodriguez, trans. *The Collected Works of St. John of the Cross*, Rev. Ed. Washington, D.C.: ICS Publications, 1991.
Ladinsky, Daniel, trans. *The Gift: Poems by Hafiz, the Great Sufi Master*. New York: Penguin Putnam Inc., 1999.
Lockey, Paul, ed. *Studies in Thomistic Theology*. Houston: Center for Thomistic Studies, 1996.
Mattingly, H. and G. R. Woodward, trans. *St. John Damascene: Barlaam and Ioasaph*. Cambridge, Mass.: Harvard

University Press, 1914. http://sunsite.berkeley.edu/ OMACL/Barlaam/

Mitchell, Stephen, trans. *Bhagavad Gita*. New York: Harmony Books, 2000.

Nash, Englund Anne, trans. *Complete Works of Elizabeth of the Trinity*, volume 2: "Letters from Carmel." Washington, D.C.: ICS Publications, 2000. www.icspublications.org/archives/index.html

Nicholson, D.H.S. *The Mysticism of St. Francis of Assisi*. London: Jonathan Cape, 1923.

Salmond, S.D.F., trans. *St. John of Damascus. Exposition of the Orthodox Faith*. Post Nicene Fathers, Schaff Edition, volume IX, series II. Aberdeen, Scotland: Free Church College, 1898.

Teresa of Avila. E. Allison Peers, trans. *Interior Castle*. New York: Bantam Doubleday Dell, 1990.

Teresa of Avila. E. Allison Peers, trans. *The Way of Perfection*. New York: Image Books, 1991.

Thérèse of Lisieux. John Clarke, trans. *Story of a Soul: The Autobiography of St. Thérèse of Lisieux*, 3rd ed. Washington, D.C.: ICS Publications, 1997.

Thorold, Algar and Harry Plantinga, trans. *The Dialogue of the Seraphic Virgin Catherine of Siena*. London: Kegan, Paul, Trench, and Trubner, 1907. Digitized by Harry Plantinga, 1994. www.ccel.org/c/catherine/dialog/dialog.html

Treece, Patricia, ed. *Quiet Moments with Padre Pio: 120 Daily Readings*. Atlanta: Charis Books, 1999.

Wilson, R. McL, trans. *The Gospel of Philip*. New York: Harper & Row, 1962.